Narcissistic Lovers

Narcissistic Lovers

How to Cope, Recover and Move On

By

Cynthia Zayn and Kevin Dibble, M.S.

New Horizon Press
Far Hills, New Jersey

New Horizon Press
P.O. Box 669
Far Hills, NJ 07931

Cynthia Zayn and Kevin Dibble, M.S.
Narcissistic Lovers
How to Cope, Recover and Move On

Cover Design: Wendy Bass
Interior Design: Susan Sanderson

Library of Congress Control Number: 2006923697

ISBN 13: 978-0-88282-283-9
ISBN 10: 0-88282-283-7
New Horizon Press

Manufactured in the U.S.A.

15   14   13   12   11   5   6   7   8   9

Acknowledgements

We would like to thank God for the opportunity to share our thoughts and sincere hopes with people who are going through difficulties in their relationships. Thanks to our families for their patience and understanding as we inundated them with information about NPD and spent time away from them as we worked on this project. We would also like to acknowledge Sam Vaknin as a major influence. His book, *Malignant Self Love: Narcissism Revisited,* offers profound insight from the perspective of a narcissist. Last but not least, our sincere thanks to the folks at "It's a Grind" coffee shop in Canton, Georgia for providing the necessary fuel and residence as we worked on final touches of this book.

Authors' Note

This book is based on research, a thorough study of the available literature and experience counseling patients, as well as clients' real life experiences. Fictitious identities and names have been given to all characters in this book in order to protect individual privacy and some characters are composites. For purposes of simplifying usage, the pronouns he/she and him/her are sometimes used interchangeably.

The information contained herein is not meant to be a substitute for professional evaluation and therapy.

Table of Contents

Introduction

The beginning of a toxic relationship can sometimes appear so alluring and promising. The destructive features of the relationship are at first elusive, and seem indefinable. Many people blame themselves in an attempt to resolve the conflict, or may question the reality of their perceptions. In many cases, by the time the "poison" of the relationship is finally detected, emotional damage has already been done, and the only feelings that remain are pain, self-doubt and confusion.

It can be hard work to recover from such a relationship without feeling permanently injured and disconnected from one's true "self." An even greater challenge is to emerge from such a painful experience with increased clarity, personal power and hope. To achieve this level of healing and to move past mere "survival first" requires, very simply, a clear picture of what happened, and the major underlying causes.

Many victims of injurious and emotionally abusive relationships were unwittingly victimized by someone with Narcissistic Personality

Disorder, an often misunderstood psychiatric condition that is character-
ized by, among other things, deceit, manipulation and complete and
utter self absorption. If you feel you may have been involved with someone with Narcissistic Personality Disorder and you are struggling to find
an explanation for what happened to you, know that this very motivation can be the source of your healing. For if you search and discover the
true nature of a Narcissistic "relationship" the understanding and clarity
you can achieve will be truly liberating.

Many readers would benefit from going through therapy as they
seek to recover and redefine their lives. This can be a very difficult
process to face alone, and an objective therapist can help sort out and
identify forces such as family dynamics, childhood experiences, and intimacy issues that influence one's perceptions, feelings and choices.
Further, many victims of Narcissists have endured emotional and/or
physical abuse, making the impact of the relationship even more damaging, and the need for therapy more certain. This book is not meant to
be a substitute for therapy, and the authors are not mental health professionals.

Since this book was written for victims of Narcissists, an "acade-
mic" writing style is avoided. The goal is to lead the reader on a personal
journey that is more than a summary of psychological theory, for true
healing of any type requires more of the reader than "intellectualizing"
the experience. A personal tone is emphasized not only to enhance the
book's readability, but to create a "writer/reader connection" that is
based on a sincere hope for personal growth and healing.

Many who have been hurt in a relationship that turned toxic without warning may have heard the terms "Narcissist," or "Narcissistic," but
may not know that they were in a relationship with a Narcissist. Confusing
the issue, the terms "Narcissist," "Narcissistic" and "Narcissism" have been
used to describe a wide variety of personality characteristics ranging from

the phrase, "a healthy Narcissism" to full-blown "Narcissistic Personality Disorder." In fact, it has been suggested by Alice Miller in *The Drama of the Gifted Child* that the term Narcissism has been so commonly used to describe such diverse meanings, "that it is difficult today to rescue it for scientific use." Nevertheless, this book attempts to describe, in laymen's terms, the complex forces at work that doom nearly all relationships with a Narcissist. In the process, a variety of terms are used that are not the authors' own, such as the "False Self" (Winnicott), or "Narcissized," (describing the experience of being victimized by a Narcissist), or "supply" (a Narcissist's "fuel" for existence). These terms are found in scholarly journals, books, or even internet discussion sites, and are commonly used to describe the condition or dynamics of Narcissism.

Though no one truly knows the ratio of male Narcissists to female Narcissists, it is generally agreed to be somewhat more prevalent with males. Nevertheless, there is no shortage of Narcissists who are women, so throughout this book, gender pronouns will be used interchangeably to reflect this fact.

Part One

Chapter 1

Are You Involved With a Narcissist?

Hello Friend,

Still feeling confused about that crazy relationship? Are things still not adding up? Let me see if I have it straight. You say things appeared to be great when you first met him or her, almost "too good to be true," right? It was uncanny how much you and your partner seemed to have in common. As a matter-of-fact, you felt you never had as much in common with any other person. Am I right?

In the beginning, he or she made you feel so appreciated. That special person complimented you by saying things like, "You are the perfect fit," "I have never had a relationship this special," "I cannot believe how much we share" and "You are the best at..." One reason these statements made you feel so significant was that your new interest told you stories of his or her previous partner who had been negative and demeaning. You were probably feeling sorry for your partner who had such an unhealthy relationship prior to you.

Not too long into the relationship, however, I'm sure your lover began to make you feel insecure. Oh…you probably didn't quite notice it at first. Perhaps there were subtle put-downs or comparisons where you weren't the one coming out on top anymore. Let me guess, some of the very things he or she used to praise you for became the things he used against you. This was confusing to you. How could you be the perfect fit, the best relationship he had ever had, his idea of a fairy tale romance, yet end up being the target of so many negative comments?

Did you ever start to wonder if you were going crazy? Did things in your relationship sometimes make absolutely no sense whatsoever? Did your partner deny saying things that you knew for a fact he/she had said? Did he/she ever accuse you of being the one telling the lie or misconstruing his/her words? If you answered "yes" to a few of these questions, it is very possible you were dating, or are still dating, a narcissist (an "N").

In this book, we will use the letter "N" to indicate the Narcissist. Sometimes, we will use the male and sometimes the female pronoun to indicate the Narcissist. Narcissists can be of either gender. Although the latest DSM study shows there to be a shift to a greater percentage of females affected by NPD, seventy-five percent of narcissists are men.

Sigmund Freud was one of the first mental health professionals to describe narcissism in pathological terms. But only in 1980 did the Diagnostic and Statistics Manual (DSM), the standard classification of mental health professionals in the United States, recognize it as a mental health category. The DSM gives diagnostic criteria and the symptoms, which have to be present so that an accurate diagnosis can be made. Over time, the psychiatric community saw Narcissistic Personality Disorder (NPD) as a disorder that could be treated but not cured. According to recent studies, the causes of NPD are not known. However, it is believed to have its origins in the early childhood years and to have been influenced by parents, peers or caregivers of those afflicted. During a particular stage of personality development, either too much or not enough attention is given to a child who then learns to "love himself" or "depend only on himself" as a means of self-preservation.

Sometimes the N shares stories about his childhood or reveals specific details about his mother which demonstrate a possible strained mother/son relationship. Do you remember your partner referring to anything out of the ordinary in regards to his/her relationship with a parent? Did he seem extremely close to his mother, or did she get on his last nerve? Either way, she could be an important piece of the puzzle you have been trying to put together.

Psychologists believe that the N spends her life trying to re-live whatever went wrong at a particular time in her personality development. She finds more and more people with whom to reenact her life and each time she truly believes "This time I will get it right." So at the onset of your relationship, she *really* did believe you were the perfect fit, the best relationship, or her ideal love. She believed those things because she wanted to believe them, she *needed* to believe them. Because the N feels unloved and insecure, she spends her life trying to find "ideal love." She believes in a perfect love that will end her search and stop her pain. She goes from relationship to relationship, sometimes without pause for recovery. This is baffling to those she leaves behind. How can she just move along like that...especially after things seemed so intense?

Is any of this "ringing a bell?" Have you wondered how your partner could just move on without blinking an eye? Have you wondered how strange it was that he/she replaced you so quickly? Or has it not reached that stage yet?

If you have experienced this part already you must be feeling heart-broken and confused. You thought you two were doing okay. Sure, there were some lows, all relationships have them, but you were willing to work them out and make things right. You thought the relationship was worth fighting for. You had way too much in common with him and at first he made you feel too special to just throw it all away. How could he tell you that you were so wonderful and then just walk away and never look back? And what about those in-between times when he said cruel things? Did you make excuses for him? You did, didn't you? You thought he wouldn't have said those things if he hadn't been under so much strain at the time, or maybe you felt as if you had provoked him into saying them.

Oh my friend, you have been completely "narcissised" and you don't even know it! Don't worry. Many people have suffered at the hands of an N and not all victims have been women. The best way to heal from this type of abuse is to become educated about the disorder. After all, knowledge is power. There are websites devoted to NPD and Internet discussion forums for victims of narcissistic abuse. Books and articles have been written about different types of Narcissists and treatments for the disorder. Most psychologists and therapists, however, tend to agree that there is no cure for NPD.

Many who study NPD believe that during an important stage of personality development for the N, a significant individual in his life needed him to be something other than what he was. The N then felt as if he had to be different in order to be loved or accepted by that individual. This is known as "narcissistic injury" and it devastates the emerging "self" of the N. Unable to be the person she truly is and still gain acceptance, the N adapts by splitting her personality into a real and a false self. The N learns to hide the "real" self because it's seen in a negative way. She tries to compensate for her "shortcomings" by creating a "special" self —a person who will be loved and admired by all. This explains why she seems to have so much in common with so many people and how she is able to voluntarily morph into different individuals.

The N becomes what the environment "needs" him to be. He also makes those around him into what he needs *them* to be. I know this seems bizarre, but think about it, it makes sense. We become mere objects to the N. He never fully experienced love the way an emotionally healthy person does and therefore merges himself with his "objects"…us. This explains why the N is unable to distinguish personal boundaries. All of the times he seemed to make himself at home, with your things or in your space, he wasn't actually feeling close to you. Instead, he was claiming it as his own, just as a toddler claims another toddler's toys by exclaiming, "MY BALL!"

Usually, the "objects" with which the N chooses to merge, have traits or characteristics that the N wishes himself to obtain. That is why he is drawn to people with strengths in certain areas. We are supposed to feel flattered when we realize that even though it seemed like chance that we were brought together, that the N actually "hand-picked" us due to particular positive characteristics or strengths that we possessed. While this knowledge may be mildly comforting, it does nothing to ease the frustrating sting of confusion and disappointment left in his wake.

Think back on the past partners of your N. Didn't they all possess certain impressive characteristics or strengths? And did you ever notice how your N would brag about someone from her past, only to cut him down in the next breath? Didn't it ever seem strange to you that she seemed to rave about certain characteristics of past boyfriends or fondly remember the times they spent together, yet have no desire to be in a relationship with them again?

Narcissistic injury (that very first incident that caused the N to split and form his "false" self) is replayed many times throughout the N's life through his relationships with others. He spends so much time building himself up and inflating his "false" self. When anyone tries to interfere with the image he has so carefully created, he experiences an injured feeling. To protect himself from that feeling, the N uses different types of defense mechanisms. One such mechanism is "devaluation." By emotionally injuring others, he protects his "false" self. That is why he felt the need to insult you or make you feel badly about yourself. Take a few moments and try to recall a time your partner insulted you or made you feel negatively about yourself. Did it follow an incident in which you had perhaps corrected him in some way or criticized him about something? Did you try to explain how he could have possibly been mistaken or that perhaps he had said something he was denying having said? When threatened in such a way, those old and familiar insecurities begin to arise. The N experiences narcissistic injury all over again. One way to crush those feelings is to devalue the person posing the threat. This gives the N a feeling of superiority and control over that person. Control... even in a false sense, is very important to the N.

At the onset of all relationships, the N feels drawn to his partner because of her special strengths and characteristics. He wants those strengths to be a part of his "false" self. He admires them and mirrors them. Anything is better than the way he truly feels about himself. He will take on her personality in bits and pieces. He doesn't even realize he is doing this. Was there ever a time when he mimicked your own words? Did you ever say something to him only to have it played back to you later as if it were his own original idea? This is very common with those afflicted with NPD. They merge so closely with their "objects" that they really seem to lose sight of where they end and their partner begins. Their partner's words become their own. Their partner's houses, cars and even friends become their own.

Once you learn the characteristics of NPD, the possibility that you had been or are still dating an N may initially seem overwhelming. On the one hand, you don't want to believe that this is or was the case. On the other hand, too much of it makes sense for you to *not* delve into the matter further.

But beware: to accept the possibility that you are dating or have dated an N means you will have to accept the fact that your partner didn't consider you "special." And you must know that he wasn't capable of "real" love. Think back on the time spent with him. You now may possibly even see it as a waste. That is always very hard to do, especially for those who have spent many years trying to cultivate relationships with N's.

Many of us find it easier to find fault within ourselves than to put any of the blame on our partners. If we are ready for a relationship, we like to believe there is a "happily ever after." We will fight to maintain or work to cultivate toward that happy ending. When we feel that is being threatened in any way, we tend to strike out with our own defense mechanisms. One of those mechanisms is denial. We find ourselves pretending things aren't the way they seem. We make excuses for our partners or believe that things will get better "when" or "if."

The fact of the matter is, if we are dating an N, things are not going to get better. Since the N views us as mere objects, we aren't loved in the traditional sense of the word. We are tools the N uses for his narcissistic supply. Narcissistic supply is anything the N can use to help promote his "false" self. He needs others to lift him, to make him feel special and to reinforce his belief that he is superior in many areas. As long as we are giving him that supply, we are considered useful to the N. Initially, he will mistakenly believe that feeling to be love. However, in reality, it is a drug…a way for him to elevate himself. And, as with all drugs, it will eventually lose it's potency. That is why the N is always in constant search for new partners (new supply, or NS).

Haven't you ever wondered why your partner seemed to scan the room every time you were in public? Maybe she told you she liked observing people and that she was into "details." Did you ever wonder why she seemed to have several male "friends" that she kept in touch with even while you were together? The N keeps supply on hand. Different people offer different supply to her. She will keep them around for as long as they continue to "buy into" her act and praise her for her "greatness." The moment they begin to see beyond the act or discontinue the praise she so desperately needs, she will discard them like an old shoe...like the objects they are to her.

Partners of the N see his inconsistencies first hand, notice contradictions and, therefore, are more apt to criticize those things. That is, when the N will feel threatened, injured and becomes defensive. The N will begin devaluing his partner in order to regain control.

Unfortunately, after the N has devalued his partner, she loses that "ideal" appeal to him and he sees her as "damaged goods." She is no longer necessary to him as supply and he begins to "discard" her by continuing the devaluation until the relationship is finally over. Many times the N will start to line up new supply (NS) months before the relationship is officially over. Some have been known to sign up on Internet dating sites while *still in relationships* with their partners. The devaluation may have been ongoing for quite some time, but the partner, viewing the relationship as "normal," thinks they are just having problems and remains willing to work things out. She usually has no clue that she is the only one working to improve the situation. Does any of this sound familiar?

Why is it so hard for us to believe we could have possibly been "narcissized?" What is it about us that would prefer to believe *we* have some flaw or have made some major mistake to cause our partner to treat us the way he/she did? The truth is the partners blame themselves rather than doubt their N's. Narcissistic Personality Disorder seems to be such a cold, malignant disease. No one wants to believe it exists...and if it does, no one wants to believe his or her partner is afflicted with a disorder which inflicts such cruelty.

N's have been compared to vampires. This analogy makes a lot of sense when breaking down the characteristics of the disorder. The vampire is considered to be damned and cursed with his fate, just as the N is cursed with his disorder. Neither the vampire nor the N willingly chose his fate. The vampire uses people as tools and sources of supply to continue his existence…his constant, futile search for deliverance. The N uses people as supply as well; he needs them to keep his "false self" alive while he continues his futile search for "ideal" love and deliverance of the disorder which enslaves him. The vampire cannot see his own image in a mirror and neither can the N. This is because the N has worked so hard to keep his real image hidden. He spent years trying to create and cultivate his "false" self; he has pieced it together from bits of supply to which he was attracted. Therefore, when he glances into a mirror, he sees his supply staring back at him. He sees a cracked and plastered vision of several people, none of which are even remotely similar to the "vile and disgusting" *real* self he has carefully hidden. Vampires are considered "soulless," doomed to roam the earth, snatching souls from innocent victims. Many people consider the N to be "soulless" because he seems to have no conscience or pity for his victims. Victims of N's often say they feel as if their soul has been raped or even robbed by the N. Like the vampire, the N seems to roam the earth acting as a victim of his own disorder, gathering supply, almost unwillingly, as he searches for some sort of cure or deliverance. Destruction of the vampire comes about when he is exposed to light, and the N will cease to exist when his "true" self is "brought to light."

Once those who are victims of N's accept the fact that their partners are afflicted with NPD, they sometimes find themselves feeling pity for the Narcissist. They refuse to believe there is no real cure for the disorder and they set out on a journey to "fix" the person. This is especially true for people with co-dependent tendencies. Co-dependents have been shaped since childhood to "fix" everything. They spend their lives and many of their relationships trying to make things right. This arrangement works perfectly for the N who seeks to be accommodated. Those who gain insight into co-dependency realize that perhaps their own parent was an N. They begin to see how they were shaped into becoming co-dependents at very early ages. Looking at the characteristics of an N, they can compare him/her to their mother or father.

According to the DSM, the N has a grandiose sense of self-importance. He will often exaggerate his achievements and expects to be recognized as superior. He believes that he is special and that only "special" people or people of high-status and importance can understand him. He believes in "ideal" love and is constantly in search of it. He has fantasies of unlimited success, power or beauty. He constantly needs admiration and praise. He has a sense of entitlement and takes advantage of others in order to achieve his own goals. He is incapable of feeling empathy and cannot identify with the needs and feelings of others. He often has a snobby attitude or comes across as arrogant. He is envious of others and believes others to be envious of him. In order to be diagnosed with an actual permanent Narcissistic Personality Disorder, five of the above criteria need to be met. Many times the N believes others are talking about him when they are not. Paranoia and bi-polar tendencies seem to be prevalent in N's, as well.

In addition, the DSM IV states, "Many highly successful individuals display personality traits that might be considered narcissistic" and that, "Only when these traits are inflexible, maladaptive, persisting and cause significant functional impairment or subjective stress, is it considered Narcissistic Personality Disorder."

Once a victim of an N realizes that her own parent could have possibly been afflicted with NPD, she begins to pull pieces of the puzzle together. Situations from her childhood that she had once thought "normal" suddenly seem not as normal when she views them as situations influenced by an N. Understanding that she could have been shaped and prepared to deal with an N as early as her childhood, the victim realizes how she was able to continue in such a relationship.

You don't have to be a co-dependent to be in a relationship with an N, but many times that is the case. A co-dependent has usually been taught to take the blame or justify odd behavior. A co-dependent will be more likely to accept negative behavior for longer periods of time while making excuses for, or actually believing that the N is going to get better at some point.

Studies have shown that N's who sometimes have relationships with other N's have a more "successful" relationship. This is because both partners use each other for supply and don't expect more from the relationship. When they need new supply they take it, while understanding that their old supply will be waiting for them when necessary.

Successful relationships with N's are those in which the partner seems to sacrifice many of the traditional expectations of a relationship. Some partners realize their N is not going to be faithful, so in order to keep the relationship together they participate in wife swapping or other types of permissive infidelities. Do you know anyone like this? Some partners of N's want to keep their relationship together so badly that they will often sacrifice their own happiness and allow themselves to stay in relationships where they have to share their partner in order to be a part of his life. The N sees this as the ultimate form of narcissistic supply because he views himself as such a wonderful person that his partner is actually willing to share him in order to keep him. If he can stay with her after that, without feeling disgust or disrespect for what he views as desperation, the relationship can continue in this fashion for as long as he allows.

Sometimes, when we study the characteristics of an N, we become paranoid that perhaps we, ourselves, are N's. However, everyone possesses a certain amount of narcissism, which is necessary for protection against certain types of emotional injury. It becomes a problem when those characteristics are so dominant that they leave no room for empathy or respect for others.

Don't worry if you are feeling a bit overwhelmed right now and if some major light bulbs are flashing in your head at this time. Sit back and take a nice, deep breath. There is actually a way for you to heal from all of this "N-fliction." Contrary to popular belief, there is a way for the N to heal as well. But first, my friend, you must piece together more of this puzzle that has recently been confusing you so much. So read on.

There is a saying that goes: "It is hard to see the forest for the trees." When we see another person's situation, we seem to know exactly what must be done. Perceptions of our own situations tend to be clouded by doubts and false hopes, whether consciously or subconsciously. So we are not always able to know exactly what to do. Hence, we often continue in hopeless relationships, repeating patterns and behaviors that secure their doom. In an effort to "clear the trees" a bit, let's look at other relationships. Perhaps you will see elements of your own relationship in one of the stories in this book. If so, it should help you gain a better understanding of N's and NPD.

Chapter 2

Seeing the Forest

Now that we have examined some of the characteristics of narcissistic men and women in chapter one, I hope you gained some understanding about NPD and insight into the possibility that you may have been "narcissized." Sometimes statistics and psychological terminology can get in the way of a clear understanding. That is why we want to share this personality study with you:

Linda's divorce had been final for three weeks and she was starting to breathe a sigh of relief. Eric, her ex-husband, had played every game in the book to make the divorce a nightmare for her. She couldn't understand why he tried to make things so difficult when he had been the one to walk away.

The first few months after their separation, Linda, who had custody of their eleven-year-old daughter, had been a wreck. Even songs on the radio seemed to taunt her. "All That's Left is a Band of Gold" seemed to target her own situation as she nervously tried to change the radio station. Looking back over her twelve-year marriage, she tried to imagine what she could have done differently. She was aware that no marriage is perfect and couples have to work hard *to stay together. Knowing she hadn't been the "perfect wife," she was willing to see a marriage counselor in order to work on their problems. Eric hadn't.*

After going through all the stages of loss from denial to anger, Linda began to accept her new life as a single mother and decided she could make it on her own without a man. Almost at the moment of her acceptance of this new decision, in walked Robert. She saw him as her reward for having been such a trooper during her separation and divorce process. Robert seemed to be everything Eric was not. Amazingly, Linda had many things in common with Robert...right down to favorite snack foods. She felt that fate had brought the two of them together, because Robert had just gotten out of a terrible relationship with a clingy, insecure woman who had been stalking him and sending him threatening letters; Linda was such an amazing contrast to her.

In the beginning of their relationship, Linda felt as if Robert's search for a perfect mate was over. According to him, she possessed every quality he had been looking for in a woman and he treated her little daughter very well. He said Linda was the exact opposite of his last partner and he almost immediately made himself at home with her and her daughter. Not even three months into the relationship Robert professed his love, and while it seemed a bit premature to Linda for "I love you's," she felt, based on the uncanny coincidences and remarkable amount of things they had in common, the emotion was well founded.

However, the honeymoon stage of their relationship quickly began to dissipate. One lazy afternoon, as Linda and Robert were lounging around her house watching movies, he made a seemingly fond comment about an old girlfriend. Linda felt the hair on her body bristle, because it came across almost as a comparison and Linda was not the one coming out on top. She decided to let the comment slide in case she had been overly sensitive about it but a few days later, a similar incident occurred. Robert had always bragged about Linda being very neat and organized, but one day he mentioned, in a sarcastic tone, that she needed to be less "anal retentive" about things. She asked herself how he could insult her about the very things to which he had once felt attracted.

As time went on, Linda noticed that Robert frequently commented on qualities she had that seemed to displease him. She found herself "jumping through hoops" trying to right all her "wrongs" and make him as happy as he had seemed in the beginning of their relationship. Nothing seemed to work. She began to feel insecure. Robert, at this point, seemed to be spending a lot of his leisure time on the computer rather than with her and didn't want to be disturbed. She did not like the way the relationship made her feel. Now she felt as if she were in competition with his past loves, loves he had complained about in the beginning of their relationship. She began wondering why Robert would ever break up with such "wonderful" women. Even women who were mere acquaintances of Robert seemed to hold some magical position of honor for him. As each new day passed, Robert became more critical and Linda felt herself falling further and further from his grace and yet, at times, they recaptured the old magic at least in her eyes.

What bothered her most was that whenever he snapped at her for what she viewed as "no particular reason," he seemed to find a way to blame it on her. There were times when she felt as if she HAD provoked him in some way. This just added to her confusion, because when she tried to respond in an opposite way, he still found fault with her. Robert seemed to expect Linda to deal with his mood swings, yet he never tolerated her moodiness.

Finally, Robert told her he was no longer happy and was ready to end the relationship. Linda was devastated. She had spent so much time trying to recapture the role she had played for Robert during the first few months of their relationship that she hadn't noticed he had given her signals that he wanted to leave. She felt she must have done something to make him feel dissatisfied, but she wasn't sure exactly what that could have been. Blaming herself, she felt if she could only figure out what she had done to change his attitude toward her, she could make things right again. She told Robert they needed to try to make things work, because their relationship was special and worth fighting for, but Robert was ready to go. He seemed disgusted with Linda's display of clingy insecurity.

After Robert left, Linda felt as if she were in some sort of emotional limbo. She spent days trying to figure out what had happened. She thought back to the early days of their relationship when she felt like a hero who had rescued Robert from his lonely quest for ideal love. Now she sat, dumbfounded and heart broken, wondering how it had all gone so wrong.

Robert didn't appear to be outwardly unhappy. In fact, there were moments just before he announced that he was leaving when he had actually seemed elated about their relationship. It didn't make any sense to her. She tried to recall any specifics that might shed some light on her dark confusion. She remembered all the time Robert had been spending on the Internet. When she would walk into the room he would minimize the screen he had been on and seem irritated that she had disturbed him. She remembered how he began taking his cell phone with him while taking out the trash and spent longer and longer amounts of time outside. If Linda questioned him about it, he became angry. Later, he always seemed apologetic and almost his old self. She had just assumed that his work was stressing him and that it was nothing personal. As soon as things settled down at work, she felt he would be the sweet man he had been when she first met him.

Even though Robert had hurt her many times, Linda had told herself it was nothing personal. He ensured her how special she was to him and that she was the woman of his dreams and everything he had ever wanted in a woman. What were a few misunderstandings or mood swings compared to that? She found herself missing his touch. Their physical relationship had been so special…a "perfect fit."

One rainy afternoon, Linda's cell phone rang and she was surprised to hear Robert's voice on the other end. He wanted to meet her to discuss some things that had been on his mind. Linda had not really moved on since Robert had broken up with her, but she was starting to awaken in the mornings without that gnawing pain in her gut.

During their meeting, Robert confessed that leaving Linda was a mistake and that the past five months had been miserable for him. He said he believed their relationship was worth fighting for. As a matter-of-fact, he used the exact words Linda had used when she tried to save the relationship before he left her. He told her that the woman he had been dating was such a nag and didn't seem to understand him. He said no one understood him the way Linda did. He told her he hadn't been able to get her off his mind and wanted a chance to make things right. If she would take him back he promised that he would spend the rest of his life making everything up to her. Linda was ecstatic. Robert had practically read her mind. Never before had anyone understood or had as much in common with her. Who could blame Robert for needing some space to clear his head? Things were too "perfect" for him with such a compatible partner. He had never met anyone like Linda before and the idea of commitment scared him into the arms of another woman, a very incompatible woman. Now he knew Linda was the perfect mate for him!

Linda took him back, yet within weeks after Robert's return, she was dealing with the familiar pangs of insults and comparisons to his past partners. Even the woman he had left to come back to Linda seemed to hold a certain amount of importance when he wasn't cutting her down for being such a nag. Things were very confusing to Linda. She did not like the person she was becoming when she was with Robert. Once again, nothing she did seemed to satisfy him. She began to feel tired just trying to "meet his standards." When her friends asked her how things were going, she lied and said they were wonderful. She didn't want anyone to know the truth. Besides, he would start treating her with more respect as soon as his job stress lessened and as soon as his ex-girlfriend refrained from calling and harassing him.

The second time Robert left, Linda didn't feel as confused as she had the prior time, although she still loved him and it hurt her to see the relationship end. The first time Robert left, Linda tried to convince him to stay. She didn't *want him to walk away from what he described as his "perfect relationship" and she felt he would regret overreacting and losing her. She had begged him not to leave. Looking back on that experience, she felt ashamed, because it made her feel desperate and clingy. This time she simply let him go. There was a numbness that prevented her from reacting. As days passed, it occurred to her that Robert must have been communicating with new women before their relationship had officially ended. That explained all his time on the Internet and all of the strange calls he received on his cell phone. Remaining in emotional limbo during round two, Linda realized she had been played. She felt angry and did not want to accept that. Only stupid people got played. She had two college degrees and ran her own business. She should have seen a player coming a mile away. Maybe he was just confused or maybe the stories he told her about his childhood prevented him from having a normal relationship. There had to be some kind of explanation. She considered herself to be relatively attractive and most men seemed only interested in her looks. But Robert initially told her she wasn't really his "type" from the beginning. She loved the fact that he had fallen in love with her in spite of not being attracted to her; it appeared to her as "real love." Could that have been part of his plan? Could he have somehow known that she wouldn't fall for the same compliments and praise that she received from other men? Had he purposely worked another angle —one that would have been more believable to her?*

Six months later, Linda realized Robert was still with the woman he had met on an Internet dating site a couple of weeks before they had broken up the second time. She felt a sting of insecurity as she wondered if this time he had actually found what he had been searching for…if this woman was the answer to his prayers for an ideal relationship. The possibility that it wasn't Robert or his childhood hang-ups that caused their relationship to end was too much for Linda. She had been secretly spying on Robert for the past six months by reading his Internet dating profiles and calling his office from pay phones just to hear his voice. She just knew he wasn't able to hang onto a woman and that his latest partner would soon be tossed to the wayside, just as she had been. However, six months had passed and all her sources informed her that Robert seemed to have finally found "the one." Linda couldn't imagine what this new woman had that was so much more appealing than what she possessed. There were times that Linda actually considered being Robert's friend just to keep him in her life in some capacity. She saw how Robert had held his "friends" in such high esteem. She imagined being the "friend" Robert sneaked off to call while taking out the trash. A part of her wanted to be the "special" one in his life while his new partner was the one doubting and questioning in a clingy way. After being the partner, however, Linda didn't wish that same pain on anyone else…even his new girlfriend. So she kept quiet and tried to stifle her humiliation, finding relief in the fact that she was better off without a boyfriend who made her feel insecure and full of doubt. Her friends kept telling her to "get over it" and move along, but she knew there was more to the situation than met the eye. Things were simply not adding up.

Chapter 3

A Familiar Story

Did any of the incidents or interchanges from Linda and Robert's story seem familiar to you? Have you experienced overwhelming acceptance and praise at the onset of a relationship, only to have it chipped away by insults, digs or comparisons? Have there been times you felt as if you were in competition with your partner's past loves or even your partner himself? Did he ever brag about himself or word things in such ways that you felt the desire to compliment or praise him?

Did you wonder at the end of your relationship how your partner could move so quickly into another one? All of these things would be out of the ordinary and bizarre if they occurred within a healthy relationship. With a Narcissist, however, all of these things are "normal."

N's don't "have" relationships with people; they are not capable. Instead, they have "interactions" with people. N's are like scriptwriters. They are constantly spinning tales and creating narratives for themselves. They tend to write characters in and out of their scenes as they see fit.

Also, N's don't feel love the way "normal" people do. What passes for love with an N is actually "narcissistic supply." Narcissistic supply is any feeling that validates the N. He must feel as if he exists. He must feel as if he is so important and that everyone around him is affected by his very presence in some way. If he can cause someone to feel anger, hate, happiness, sadness or any type of emotion, he experiences feelings of control and gets a rush. That "rush" is the N's "love."

If your partner doesn't possess at least five of the criteria for NPD listed earlier, chances are you are not dealing with an N. Narcissistic Personality Disorder can easily be misdiagnosed. Some cultures condition males to treat females in ways that Western Society might view "narcissistically." Therefore, cultural factors need to be taken into consideration before assuming the worst. Regardless of intention, if you feel victimized you have a right to demand respect. Besides, learned behaviors such as "machismo" are often part of particular cultures' expectations for males and can be *unlearned*.

Based on the information you have been learning about NPD, if you believe you have been "narcissized," you may be experiencing the humiliation of having been "played." Don't. First of all, being "narcissized" is completely different from being "played." The difference deals with "intent." The difference between a player and an N is that the N *really does* believe he has found the perfect mate or "ideal love" at the onset of each new relationship. N's are often compared to alcoholics or drug abusers (as a matter-of-fact, it is said that not all N's are alcoholics, but all alcoholics are N's). To an N, his new partner is like a new drug. The possibility that this is "the one" or that he has finally found "ideal love" is what gives him such a high from his new supply (NS).

As we stated earlier, knowledge really is power. By arming yourself with this new information, you can avoid similar pain in the future. We promise! Your Nar-dar is going to be so strong that by the time you fin-ish this book you will practically be able to spot an N a mile away!

Don't Hate the "Player," Hate the Game
Has your mind been reeling with possibilities? I bet it has. By now you have probably diagnosed twenty acquaintances and relatives with NPD! That is natural, as you first become aware of this condition. Movie stars and politicians usually head up the list of possible N's at the onset of NPD discovery. Don't worry. You aren't being paranoid. You won't always see narcissistic traits in everyone, but many people can have a few of these traits without being a full blown narcissist. Knowledge is just fresh for you right now. You will become more discerning as you learn more and understand more about what exactly to look for.

As we discussed earlier, the N's partner to him or her is like an object, a shiny new car or tool. Just as a new car eventually loses its "newness" and that initial appeal, so does the NS. Oftentimes, before the relationship has officially ended, N's are already lining up new supply. They have such a subconscious fear of abandonment, due to the origin of their disorder, that they cannot be alone. Narcissists will make sure they have NS before they totally leave the old supply (OS).

More than likely, in the case of Linda and Robert, Robert had secured some NS on the internet through dating sites before breaking things off with Linda. He needed to make sure he had some NS waiting for him before he actually left Linda, because N's cannot be alone. They need their supply and often keep information about finding new and dif-ferent types close at hand. Once Robert started dating his NS and she didn't prove to be the kind of supply he needed (perhaps she didn't praise him enough or didn't see him in the way he had tried to proj-ect...or needed some attention for herself), he evidently left her and tried to return to Linda. To an N, old supply is better than no supply at all. Once an N has devalued his supply, she is practically worthless to him. If she allows him back after he has devalued and discarded, he loses any respect he may have ever had for her. But when he is in-between supply, an N will often find himself going back to his old stomping grounds, just as a drug addict or alcoholic will choose a weaker form of what he/she is craving when what he/she usually takes is not available.

Some alcoholics will even drink vanilla extract just to get a taste of alcohol when there aren't any alcoholic beverages in the house. They will feel ashamed that they had to resort to that substance, but will take what they can get until something "better" comes along. For an N, his NS isn't necessarily a "better" partner. She isn't necessarily better educated or more attractive, she is just "new." The "newness" is what makes her special to him. When an N is in-between supply, he becomes desperate, just as an addict does, and will do or say anything to get his "fix."

At that point, he goes crawling back to his OS. Robert begged Linda to take him back after he realized his NS wasn't giving him what he needed, but to Robert, Linda was like vanilla extract is to an alcoholic. He was ashamed that he had to resort to her. He knew eventually he would have some NS lined up and would be able to make his exit, but until that time came he would take what he could get from her.

When Linda took Robert back, it reinforced his belief that he was special. Unfortunately, it made Linda seem desperate and insecure in his eyes. N's are attracted to strength and independence, the very opposite traits of their "true" selves. Even when the N is the one who influenced his partner's weakness or insecurity, he only sees her newly developed negative traits, not their origin, and is disgusted by them. Robert couldn't stay too long with Linda upon his return because he saw her as a desperate woman who had no self respect when she took him back. The N's shiny new car or toy had a defect, it had lost its "newness," perhaps it was even "wrecked," it had depreciated in his mind and he was hungry for a new toy. He needed a new "object" to "love"… a new "drug."

Linda, believing Robert had seen the error of his ways, prided herself on being a compassionate person who had enough love in her heart to forgive the man with whom she was meant to be and give him another chance to right his wrongs. She didn't feel as if she were lowering her self-esteem by taking him back, because he had been the one to beg for a second chance. She had felt sympathetic toward him and wanted to make him feel better. She knew he felt terrible about leaving her and that he had learned his lesson by getting together with the "wrong woman," so she was willing to work things out and was able to continue cultivating a stronger relationship.

In well functioning relationships, when couples make mistakes and forgive each other, it makes their relationship stronger. But it is impossible to forgive and move on in a "relationship" with an N. The N views the relationship as being tainted and feels he needs to continue his quest for "ideal love" once a mistake has been made (even if it is the N's infidelity). Once the toy is broken, it is tossed aside like the useless object it has become and the N begins his search for something new…a useful object.

At this point, you may be feeling pity for your N as you realize she is at the mercy of her disorder. Compassion is evidently one of your positive traits or you wouldn't have ended up with an N in the first place. Compassion is a noble trait; it sets you apart from the N whose emotions are merely self-centered reactions. However, it is important that you do not allow yourself to be led by your emotions. Once you arm yourself with knowledge, you can choose not to be manipulated and disrespected. There is such a peace in that type of security. There is more you need to know about the emotions of an N so that you will be better equipped to handle those frustrating and confusing situations. For now, you may want to reflect upon the "object" type love of an N and her ongoing journey to find completion. Don't be discouraged. You can and will gain the knowledge to choose a partner and find the right relationship, the one for which you yearn and deserve.

Supply by Any Other Name...
While pondering the "object" type love the N chooses, you will come to understand one reason the N seems to move seamlessly from one relationship to another. We all tire of our material possessions and upgrade them from time to time. When we replace worn out objects like cell phones that no longer work, we don't grieve for the ones we discarded.

N's are said to have the emotional maturity of a five-year-old child. That is why the "toy" analogy seems to work so well when explaining their attitude toward their partners. When Linda allowed Robert to continuously cut her down and compare her to his past lovers, he lost respect for her. If she complained about the comparisons or got upset, he considered her insecure or weak and *still* lost respect for her. No matter how she reacted to his "game," she was set up to be devalued in Robert's eyes, because that was the only way he knew how to play.

N's assume that everyone thinks the same way they do about things. They are incapable of experiencing empathy or any of the emotions associated with relating to the feelings of others. The only feelings they are known to experience are ones involving their own narcissistic injury. They can experience anger, disgust, humiliation or embarrassment. They are able to feel shame and disappointment. They even feel a rush when things go their way, when they feel in control or gain supply. But they do not know what it is to feel love in the way normal people do, and they cannot feel empathy with others. They usually learn how to react by watching others and they write those reactions into the scripts they act out on a daily basis. They can mimic sorrow or sympathy, but those who understand the disorder know that those emotions are not sincere when expressed by N's.

Chances are when Robert was with his NS, he told her what a horrible partner Linda had been. While he was whispering what a perfect fit the new woman was or how he had finally found the girl of his dreams, he didn't mention to her that he had once told Linda the exact same things. Linda was surely painted as a clingy, insecure ogre, someone who wouldn't let him go (N's often like to make it appear as if their past lovers cannot get enough of them and won't leave them alone. We are almost convinced that when the ex-partner continues to contact the N in order to gain some sort of closure to the confusing madness she experienced with him, that the N actually views it as stalking) and no doubt the NS felt pity for Robert for having dated such a "freak."

What should Linda do if Robert comes back for round three? Having read this book most will say Linda will under no circumstance take him back. When we see the relationship from another person's perspective, it is easy to realize how a reunion with such a person would be a mistake. We may find it impossible to believe that someone would be willing to continue a relationship with a partner who constantly devalues her. But there are women and men who take their partners back even after being devalued and discarded several times. Many things factor into their reasons for this. Some of these people are codependents who seem to be at the mercy of their own disorder. Others are addicted to their partners and need them under any circumstance. Sometimes victims are momentarily blinded by the fog of deceit created by the N's and need only to have the air cleaner to see more distinctly. In this book we hope to teach you how to discern the truth about your own vulnerability and how you've been affected by your narcissistic lover.

QUIZ # 1
Degrees of Co-dependency

Rate your level of co-dependency from one through four.

> 4 = Often
> 3 = On occasion
> 2 = Rarely
> 1 = Never

__1__ Afraid of being alone

__2__ Feel the need to take care of the emotional needs of others

__4__ Hard on yourself

__43__ Tend to go above and beyond what you can handle

__2__ Feel the need to be needed

__1__ Need approval and appreciation from others

__3__ Majority of relationships were unhealthy

__32__ Don't give yourself the credit you deserve

__2__ Look for sources outside of yourself to gain happiness

Total __20__

   Add your score total. Scores should range anywhere from 9 through 36. A total score between 28 and 36 reflects that you have excessive co-dependent qualities. A score between 18 and 27 indicates that you have a significant amount of co-dependent traits. A score between 9 and 17 illustrates that you have a limited amount of co-dependent characteristics.

Despite the seeming need for companionship, relationships of the N are doomed. Because of the N's poor-self image, he feels that if anyone is willing to accept him as a partner she must be inferior in some way. Therefore, he cannot stay with anyone who would accept the likes of him into her life. In the beginning of the courtship, he is attracted to his partner's strengths and drawn to her confidence. Those "unobtainable" qualities are what make him pursue her, at first. He believes she could be "the one" and he also tries to convince her of this. However, once he has acquired her, and the newness begins to wear off, he believes she must be flawed in some way in order to stay with someone like him. Then he perceives flaws which are in reality his own. He grows bored, disgusted, and begins to search for NS. Unable to face his own inadequacies and give to another, he looks for another "perfect" match, continuing the self-defeating cycle of despair.

The N devalues her sources of supply, because she resents them for the power they have over her. Without supply, the N will cease to exist and learn to resent her dependency upon her supply. By devaluing the very supply on which she feels dependent, the N gains back some of the control she feels she has lost.

Negative attention equals positive attention (supply) for an N. Therapists encourage victims of N's to abide by the "No Contact" rule when dealing with break ups from their narcissistic companion. But many victims feel the way Linda seemed to feel; they doubt themselves and give the N second and third chances. Victims believe that the N really wants to change and their compassion to be the better person and offer him forgiveness overrides any feelings of resentment. However, this "forgiveness" is not as compassionate and self-sacrificing as it may seem.

Remember, as you've learned earlier when the N initiates the relationship, he convinces his partner that she is very *special*. She believes that she is "the one he has been searching for." All of the coincidences and things she had in common with her partner proved to her that theirs was more than just an average relationship. The way he made her feel in the beginning of their courtship reinforced her belief that they were made for each other and that they had a truly special relationship. Those special feelings she experienced are similar to the feelings the N has about his "false" self. His "real" self was so repulsive to him that he created a wonderful version of himself to be admired and loved by all. The feelings he received when others accepted him as the new and improved self were the actual "high" feelings obtained from his supply. When he convinced his partner that she was the special woman of his dreams, she, too, got to experience the "high" of believing in a special self. To accept that her partner didn't really believe those things about her meant she would have to give up the belief that she was "the one," and she would lose that special status. The pain that comes from having to let that "special" self go is overwhelming. That is why the N is at the mercy of his disorder and one of the reasons his partner is reluctant to let go. If his current partner begins to see through the façade he has so carefully created for himself, the "false" self is threatened. He no longer feels as if his partner is reflecting the image he wished to portray. In that case, he needs to find new supply to mirror his "false" self before reality sets in and causes him to dwell on the possibility that he isn't special, after all. If an N is forced to dwell on that possibility for too long, he often experiences depression.

When the victim of an N feels the special image his partner helped create for him being threatened, he often resorts to denial in order to hang on to his own "false self." He would much rather believe that he is the special person she made him out to be and that she is just a normal woman dealing with stress that causes her to behave inappropriately, than to believe that he could have been "narcissisized."

This is one of the reasons that victims of N's find it difficult to adhere to the "No Contact" rule. They don't see themselves as mere objects for the N. They are still clinging to the belief that they were special to the N at one time and that their N will soon get past whatever is causing her to stray and once again find refuge in their ideal relationship.

Unfortunately, the N doesn't see her supply as "special." Partners of N's are only tools she uses to buffer her feelings of guilt, anxiety and shame acquired during her childhood from her parents or other such caregivers. Once the tools are of no use to the N, she simply discards them and searches for something more useful. She doesn't desire to be loved by her supply; would someone want her car to adore her? Instead, she extracts adoration, praise, fear, admiration, and any worthwhile supply until she feels it is depleted. Then she obtains a fresh supply.

Think about it. Wasn't the beginning of your relationship almost like a fairytale? Your N made you feel so significant. He even convinced you that you two were made for each other. You had so many things in common with him. And wasn't it uncanny how none of the other women in his past measured up to you? You began to realize just how special you really were. Perhaps you *were* meant to be together. Buying into the idealization phase is a rush. Once we allow ourselves to feel as if we have rescued someone from a long and difficult journey, there is no turning back. We *want* to be that savior. We want ours to be the *best relationship* or the *most important time* in his life. Accepting that we have been "narcissized" means denying our special status. We tend to grow accustomed to that *special* side of ourselves. Why would we give that up without a fight?

The reality is that we really are special. We have all of those traits that initially drew the N to us, but he exaggerated them during the idealization phase of our relationship and we also eventually found ourselves believing in the idealizations. The malignant power the N seems to have over his victim distorts reality. This is why the victim of an N may find herself being talked into reconciliation even though something tells her it isn't right. This is one reason the "No Contact" rule is so important.

One of the reasons therapists encourage victims of N's to abide by the "No Contact" rule is that any type of attention...anger, fear, sadness, happiness, is considered equal as supply to the N. When an N is in-between supply, she may consider going back to her OS (old supply) to get a "quick fix." If he accepts her back, she will remain with him until she lines up new supply. If he expresses anger or tries to explain to her why he isn't going to take her back, he is *still* giving her supply.

The fact that he could evoke anger in her reinforces his belief in his control over others and his power of existence. The best way to handle an N when he comes sniffing back around for supply is to ignore him completely. That is the only weapon against narcissism. N's thrive on attention, whether it is positive or negative. It reminds them that they exist and that others notice them. When N's are ignored, their very existence is threatened. Although it is sometimes hard to ignore the phone calls, block the emails and send back the unopened gifts or letters, you now know it is the only way to begin the healing process. By abstaining from contact you are showing your ex-partner that he no longer has control over you. The only reason he will continue to come back and dip into old supply is if you reveal your vulnerabilities or weaknesses in those areas. When he sees your strengths and realizes you are serious, he will move onto easier supply and you will finally be free of your N.

How do you think Linda handled Robert after he devalued and discarded her *twice*? We'll soon discuss in detail exactly what she did. But first take some time to evaluate your own situation and process more of this information.

QUIZ # 2
Degrees of Narcissism

Rate the level of Narcissism you feel your partner possesses on a scale of one through four.

4 = Often
3 = On occasion
2 = Rarely
1 = Never

3 Very competitive
4 Manipulative
4 Misleads and lies
4 Insensitive to your feelings
3 Controls you
4 Envious
3 Needs to be the center of attention
4 Demeaning
4 Self-Absorbed
4 Easily angered when confronted
4 Indirectly looks for attention
4 Feels their needs take priority over yours
2 Critical of your friends
1 Careless and impulsive

Total 48

Add your score total. Scores should range anywhere from 14 through 56. A total score between 43 and 56 reflects that your partner has excessive narcissistic qualities. A score between 29 and 42 indicates that your partner has a high amount of narcissistic traits. A score between 14 and 28 illustrates that your partner has a limited amount of narcissistic characteristics.

Chapter 4

The Truth Can Set You Free

As time passed, Linda began to understand she was much better off being alone than being with someone who constantly criticized and made her feel so negatively about herself. Nevertheless, she could not get past the nagging feeling of missing Robert. Sex had been amazing with him and she had attributed that to the fact that they were meant for each other. Night after night, she sat alone in her bedroom trying to convince herself that she did not miss him and was not longing for his touch...but she did. Images of Robert touching his new partner kept flashing through her mind, giving her gut a mocking twist.

Throwing herself into caring for her daughter and her work, Linda managed to keep her mind busy during the day; as the months wore on she actually began to wake most mornings without feeling tearful and depressed. After work one day she accepted an invitation to go out for a drink with Carrie and a few other colleagues. And that decision changed her life forever.

Carrie had worked with Linda for years, though they had hardly spoken before that evening. But somehow as they sat together, Linda suddenly felt the other woman's compassion and began to confide in Carrie about her relationship with Robert. Listening intently, Carrie seemed to take everything in. Then she said, "Linda, you just dodged a big ole' bullet, girl. Robert sounds like a type A Narcissist." Linda sat in amazement as Carrie rattled off common phrases used by Narcissists, and realized Robert had used many of those exact phrases with her.

Carrie described how she had actually been "narcissized" by two men and had even sought counseling to help with her recovery. Carrie told Linda to call her whenever Linda felt herself slipping from the resolve to distance herself from Robert. Carrie told Linda, "It's hard to break that old attraction." She was more than happy to share the sound advice with Linda.

After that night, Linda decided to delve more deeply into NPD and read everything she could get her hands on that involved narcissism and the disorder. The more she studied, the more similarities she saw in her experiences with Robert and the information she was digesting. "No Contact" was advised in every article or book she read concerning what to do after a break up with a Narcissist. She began to understand why it was so important to ignore Robert and keep him out of her life. She made up her mind to do just that.

Despite her new knowledge, Linda still found herself longing for Robert at times, just as Carrie had predicted. When she felt these emotional tugs, she called Carrie to get support. Carrie explained to her that she wasn't longing for "Robert" but for the false "self" Robert had tried to project. "You are actually mourning the loss of a mirage," Carrie said. "It is hard for you to get over this because you are grieving the loss of someone who doesn't really exist." Carrie knew Linda felt intense emotions about the idea of Robert with another woman, so Carrie tried to give her an exercise that would ease her mind. Carrie said, "I want you to visualize your Narcissist sitting on the curb in front of your house. Moments later the rumble of a garbage truck is heard in the distance. Two men jump off the truck (go ahead and make them very attractive...after all, it is a fantasy) but before they can toss him in the back with the rest of the trash a woman happens by and "rescues" him from your curb. People go through other *people's trash all the time. They seem to think they can make good use out of something that someone else has thrown away. When you see someone taking a broken toaster or a worn out pair of sneakers from your trash can, you don't chase her down, do you? Besides, most of the time they eventually realize it is useless, and it ends up on their own curb a little while later."*

Linda knew Carrie had a point...still she couldn't seem to stop being bothered by the dissolution of what had once seemed a dream relationship and couldn't help herself from missing Robert. She told Carrie only half joking she wished there could be a law that required people with personality disorders to wear some sort of identity label to prevent others from becoming involved with them. Carrie said, "Once you learn how to recognize the characteristics of people with NPD, that will be all the identification you need. Trust me, now I see them coming a mile away. When something is not useful to you in a positive way, or if it is harmful to you, THROW IT AWAY."

People with a history of abusive relationships tend to remain in such situations because that is "what they know." The bizarre cat and mouse games (the praise and devaluation process) played by the abuser and his victim are familiar and even comforting to the victim in some strange way. The unusual feelings associated with non-abusive relationships leave the victim feeling panicked and longing for the familiarity associated with his/her usual (abusive) relationships. This type of behavior is referred to as "Stockholm Syndrome," after a 1973 kidnapping incident that occurred in Stockholm, Sweden. In that incident, after being kidnapped and subjected to brainwashing for a period of time, the victims resisted rescue attempts and even when rescued, they refused to testify against their captors. Stockholm Syndrome occurs when captives begin to identify with their captors, initially as a defense mechanism, and view any act of kindness, however small, in a magnified way. The syndrome has been observed in battered spouses, abused children and prisoners of war. Whether this was the reason Linda continued to long for

Robert, or not, she now realized it was not healthy to miss someone who had treated her so badly and she was determined to initiate new behavior patterns and to learn more about the destructive ones she had experienced.

Continuing her studies, Linda learned there are actually two types of Narcissists, the "Cerebral Narcissist" and the "Somatic Narcissist." She decided that Robert was a Somatic Narcissist. Somatic Narcissists use their bodies to obtain their narcissistic supply. They often work out and stay in great physical shape. They enjoy getting attention for their bodies and since they are incapable of feeling love, they use their partner's bodies as tools for masturbation rather than "lovemaking." To his partner, sex with the Narcissist is a beautiful love-making experience. But to the N, it is just another way of satisfying himself.

The N considers his partners to be extensions of himself...a way to "act out" a fantasy. Partners are interchangeable and easily discarded. Somatic Narcissists brag about their sexual conquests, expect praise for their muscular bodies, are often health nuts and some are even hypochondriacs. They rely on their looks or strength to obtain supply and learn how to please a woman by gathering experience from their many sources of supply. This is the reason sex with a Somatic Narcissist may be incredible compared to sex with a less experienced partner.

Linda thought of all the partners Robert had admitted having during his college days and beyond. She hadn't thought much of his revelations when he first told her; after all, many men are somewhat promiscuous in their single days. Looking back, however, Linda realized that Robert seemed to have had many sex partners, whom he criticized by talking many times of their shortcomings.

Thinking back, Robert's passion for weightlifting seemed more like an obsession. The way he refused to eat certain foods, even when her friends had made them special dinners, this obsession with eating properly seemed like something other than a healthy eating habit. She remembered how he would stare at himself in the mirror admiringly seemingly unable to look away when he stepped out of the shower. At the time she saw that as confidence, but now studying NPD, she noticed this to be a character trait for a Somatic Narcissist. She felt proud of him for wanting to be photographed by a professional photographer while doing muscle poses... now she just felt sick. Her earlier image of Robert's confidence now seemed traceable to a characteristic of a personality disorder to her. She was learning to view him in a completely different light.

Cerebral Narcissists use their intellect to impress others and gain supply. They are not often interested in sex and will withhold it to punish their partners. Linda learned that all Narcissists have cerebral and somatic qualities, but tend to lean toward one type more than the other.

Pieces of the puzzle slowly began to fall into place. Linda felt a sting of pain for Robert because from what she had learned, there was no real cure for the disorder. After learning more about the disorder, and remembering that Robert had confessed to such a strained relationship with his mother, Linda wanted to go to him and hold him. She wanted to tell him, "I know what is wrong with you. I am here to help you. I will make it better," but she realized that she had ALWAYS done that. She always tried to "fix" things and make them better. And Robert's real problem was something she could not fix.

As Linda's friendship with Carrie strengthened and her studies continued, so did Linda's knowledge of NPD. Linda no longer cringed every time she heard her cell phone ringing. She didn't expect to hear from Robert, nor did she associate ringing phones or new emails with him. Slowly, she was feeling stronger; not healed, but stronger. Several months passed since she had seen Robert and he did not try to contact her. She had learned the term "N-dipping" from Carrie and understood it to be when victims of Narcissists couldn't forget them and tried to find out what was happening to their ex-loves by checking their dating profiles on the internet or driving past their houses to see if they were home. N-dipping fell into the category of "contact" and was considered a major mistake. Linda learned to refrain from it.

Then one day when she was checking her email, Linda noticed a new message with the subject "Long time no see." She didn't recognize the address and had blocked Robert's email as Carrie had suggested, so she knew it couldn't be from him. She was wrong. He created another email address in order to send her the message. He wasn't begging her back this time, only telling her he was thinking of her because he knew her birthday was coming up and wanted her to know he remembered. Linda was livid. Her heart was pounding as she quickly dialed Carrie's cell phone. "After all these months how could he still have this kind of affect on me? How rude of him to just casually send me an email!"

Carrie helped Linda calm down and explained to her that Robert was more than likely beginning to grow bored with his NS and was probably hoping Linda would step back in until he found "better" supply. He hadn't begged her back this time, because he knew she would be less likely to accept him since he discarded her twice. He was "testing the waters." Due to Linda's new knowledge about NPD, it made complete sense to her and she began to feel angry. She told Carrie she intended to tell Robert she knew exactly what his problem was and that she was no longer going to serve as narcissistic supply for him. "By doing that," Carrie explained, "you will be giving him the very supply you wish to deny him." Linda knew this was an apt diagnosis from what she had studied, but she felt helpless. Robert would interpret the anger, the lecture or even the declarations of refusal as narcissistic supply.

Feelings of helpless frustration stayed with Linda throughout the day and by the time she left work she felt emotionally drained.

When she arrived home, her ex-husband was already there to take their daughter for the weekend, but her daughter hadn't arrived home from school, yet. Linda felt more tension building inside her, in her ex-husband's presence. He seemed annoyed and angry that the school bus was late and made sarcastic comments to Linda.

After he finally left, daughter in tow, Linda had a quick meltdown sitting with her head in her arms at her kitchen table. As she reflected, she flashed back *to her relationship with her ex-husband. Did her ex-husband have narcissistic tendencies? How had she never noticed those characteristics before? Was the pacifying she had done in that relationship why she had been able to stay with Robert so long? Had she learned how to survive with an N by living twelve years with one?*

Linda felt as if she had hit an all time low. When she stared at herself in the mirror she felt a pathetic person was staring back. Linda had not yet processed that through knowledge and behavior she was changing and would change more and for the better. In order to make these changes however, Linda needed to learn exactly what had gone wrong so she could grow stronger and create a better relationship in the future.

Does Linda's situation ring familiar? Have you noticed that you seem less confident and at peace with yourself than you did when you first met your N? Do you see how his constant devaluation could have lowered your self-esteem? Do you feel you are gaining insight into your own personality at this point?

Be confident. All of these painful revelations are working together to mold you into a better, stronger, wiser you. Pressure is always necessary when creating something positive. A lump of coal must endure pressure in order to become a diamond. Muscles have to rip before muscle growth is obtained. You have probably heard the saying, "No pain no gain." That truism can be applied to the epiphanies experienced by an awakening NPD victim. We promise you, the emotional roller coaster ride you are experiencing taking you from revelation to anger and disgust will end at a peaceful place if you follow the tracks.

Chapter 5

Trolling for Supply...

Please be hopeful. You are arming yourself with some powerful knowledge. If you don't feel your new strength yet, we are confident you soon will. Let's continue this journey together. There is a lot more to learn.

When things seem to be going right in the life of an N, he doesn't need his supply. His partner becomes unnecessary, as he feels no reason to be uplifted and needs no one to blame for his problems. Because the N feels "special," he expects others to appease him when things do not go his way. In his mind, people are there as amulets to cheer, encourage and support him as he continues his journey through life. He doesn't see them as individuals who need their own emotional support or who have their own paths to travel. That is why he feels confused if they refuse to cater to his needs or if they express the desire for support in their own lives.

The N must be the center of everyone's life and if he is not, he simply has no use for them. Perhaps you remember when you tried to vent to your N your feelings about a problem only to have him "one up you?"

Perhaps you told him about how someone had treated you rudely and rather than responding with sympathy or support, your N told you of a time he was treated worse than that.

Even though his supply is only measured in ways that are beneficial to the N, he still realizes its value in relation to his existence. That is why he will sometimes go to extreme lengths to assure that no one will rob him of this supply before he is ready to dispose of it. N's have been known to devalue their own partners to others...telling of their partners' instabilities and even acting like martyrs as they explain the difficulties they have had to endure while staying in such rocky relationships. Many times they are mirroring the feelings of their partners when they express such things, using their partner's words as their own. They feel it is necessary to make their partner appear undesirable to others in order to assure their partner's utter dependence upon them or to gain support and understanding from others when they decide to leave the relationship. After all, the N thrives on approval. Once again, bring to mind the analogy of the toddler-mentality which can be used in comparison; the child no longer wants his toy, but doesn't want anyone else to have it either. He licks the cupcake before putting it back on the plate.

The insecurities of the N are what lead her to rid her partner of outside interference. To an N, the friends and even family members of her partner, pose a threat of exposing her "real" self. Sometimes an N will insult her partner's friends or family or even forbid him to have relationships with them due to their "negative traits." Her partner, wanting to please her, will cut ties with those closest to him, making the N the center of his existence. Once the N has succeeded in eliminating all other outside forces, the chances of her partner becoming totally dependent upon her are greatly increased.

Remember as you learn more about the narcissistic personality, just because your N may not possess every narcissistic trait or quality does not mean he isn't afflicted with NPD. Nor does the fact that he shares some NPD characteristics make him a Narcissist. At this stage, this diagnosis is only one of the possibilities. As you continue to read, it is our hope that you will gain understanding of those possibilities in the personality of the person who has caused you much pain, and that you will also become increasingly self-aware as you acquire knowledge necessary for your recovery.

In her reading, Linda came across the term "trolling" as an explanation of how N's often search for NS. Linda discussed it with Carrie who explained that "trolling" was actually a fishing term that described how fishermen used nets, which were dragged behind their boats in order to catch fish. When an N is desperate for supply, he seems to "troll" for it rather than to carefully select it based on admirable qualities the way he normally does.

Linda, reflecting on her dysfunctional relationship, now realized that Robert's email had been a troll for supply and it made her physically sick. She desperately wanted to believe Robert was a normal guy who just had commitment issues. There were times she still missed him and wanted to be with him even as she learned more about NPD and was realizing she could never have a normal relationship with him.

Carrie suggested that Linda make a list of the negatives she had experienced in the relationship. Linda's list was two pages long. She often took it out and read through it when she felt pangs of loneliness for Robert. Sometimes, she added things to the list that she had forgotten or had recently realized as negatives. This is a good time for you to list relationship negatives. Make your own list using Linda's as a sample. Here is Linda's list:

- *Stared at other women when he was in public with me (blatantly)*
- *Compared me to women in his past, even friends, and they were always the "winners"*
- *Bragged about himself: Mentioned that he looked very young for his age, said his body looked better than some men half his age, bragged*

about his grades in college, his sporting activities, his modeling
days…

- *Constantly tried to make me feel insecure…told me ways to tone my*
  arms…said I needed to be more positive…pretended that I wasn't his
  "type" of woman so I wouldn't feel "good enough" for him and I
  would always feel appreciative that he would stay with me in spite of
  that!
- *Always put his friends before me*
- *Most of his "friends" were women*
- *Loved surfing the internet for supply*
- *Cannot be proud of any partner he has because he has to be the one*
  to come out on top
- *Felt jealous and competitive of me*
- *Cannot remain faithful to one woman*
- *Fear of commitment*
- *Cannot be trusted*
- *Unethical*
- *Changed the rules to accommodate himself*
- *Shallow*
- *All for "show"*
- *Insecure*
- *Lies come way too easily for him*
- *Made me feel inadequate*
- *Clung to newly formed "friendships" in a scary way*
- *Made excuses as to why he was late*
- *Didn't always answer his cell phone when he knew I was calling*
- *Lied about his cell phone being in his car when I called*
- *Doesn't seem to feel guilty about treating people the way he does*
- *Blamed everyone else for the negatives in his life*
- *Is constantly searching for new supply*

- *Sometimes he would just snap and go off (narcissistic rage...supposedly common with the disorder)*
- *Told me I misinterpreted what he said or that he was joking and that I just didn't understand him and was hypersensitive*
- *He is a taker*
- *Told me he didn't say things that I know for a fact he DID say*
- *Trolled for supply*

How many things on this list can you place a check by concerning your N? What other things can you add?

As Linda continued re-evaluating her experiences with Robert, she learned that when Robert denied saying things that she was certain he had said, this was called "gaslighting," a term that originated from a classic movie entitled "Gaslight," starring Ingrid Bergman. In the film, Bergman's character's husband was trying to make her think she was going insane. He would cause the lights in their house to flicker or lose brightness when he turned on the attic lights, while secretly searching for his wife's family jewels. When his wife would question him about the lights he would tell her she was imagining things. She thought she was losing her mind because she KNEW the lights were changing; yet, her husband didn't seem to notice them at all. N's tend to gaslight their victims as a way to gain control over them. However, due to the fact that N's are constantly creating narratives for themselves, they sometimes forget what they have actually said and aren't always purposely trying to make their partners feel confused. Their stories and lives are ever changing, making it difficult to remember which tale they have told.

Looking back Linda recalled how once Robert told Linda that she was the most special woman he had ever met. Several months later, she reminded him of his words and he said, "I never told you that." She couldn't believe he had forgotten something as important as that. There were many other incidents where

Robert seemed to conveniently forget things he had told her. He seemed really sincere with his denials so Linda, still doubting her own memories, wondered if she had misheard him.

As time passed in faltering moments, Linda would take out the list she made of Robert's negative attributes. Reading the list again helped Linda feel less lonely and even relieved that she wasn't still with Robert. She wondered what it was like for Robert's new partner. She knew now a Narcissist does not change his behavior patterns. Therefore, she knew it would only be a matter of time before Robert would be D&D'ing his new partner and looking for NS. After all, he had already been trolling for supply when he sent the email to her. Linda couldn't feel envious of Robert's new partner when she realized the woman was probably being devalued and made to feel insecure. She imagined Robert and his new partner in a restaurant. Robert was checking out every woman who walked past them as his partner longed for him to only have eyes for her. Linda knew all too well the sinking feeling his partner would experience as Robert compared her to his past lovers, possibly, even at times, to Linda. She did not envy the rage Robert's partner would have to experience when things weren't going his way, or the gaslighting... or the endless taking, taking, taking. Robert's new partner was undoubtedly very tired at this point, yet, clinging to the relationship since it was so "special."

The realization that Robert was only repeating his destructive relationship pattern with someone else helped Linda cope and learn to move from her depression. The knowledge that she was definitely much better off alone than in a relationship with Robert added to her feeling of becoming stable. Linda wondered how she could ever miss Robert or grieve over such a one-sided relationship. However, despite these glimmers of hope, at other times she still had feelings of despair. Those early feelings of "finally seeing the light" are sometimes described as "false empowerment" or "false breakthroughs," because while they seem to transcend all other despondent emotions or thoughts, they still can be replaced by sadness or longing with the provocation of a single memory. Unfortunately, Linda was soon to discover this for herself.

Chapter 6

Letter to a Narcissist

Carrie told Linda that her therapist had suggested that she write a letter (one she would never send) to her N to help her gain closure from their relationship. Narcissists rarely provide their partners with closure, because they usually flee from their relationships (even relationships that seem to be healthy to their partners) without looking back. Carrie encouraged Linda to write Robert such a letter to aid her healing and help gain closure.

Linda's thoughts:

> *Dear Robert,*
>
> *This is a very difficult letter to write, because I still feel very raw emotionally, but I also feel it needs to be written.*
>
> *When I first met you, I honestly thought you were the answer to my prayers, and that we were the answer to each other's prayers. You told me that you had never felt the way you felt about me with any other woman. You said we were a "perfect fit" and that you felt closer to me than you had ever felt to anyone. I sincerely believed you.*

You said you treated me with more respect than any other man had ever treated me; where did you get that information? No man has ever treated me the way you did. You made me feel worthless and inadequate. You continuously compared me to your past lovers. You seemed to look back on relationships from fifteen years ago as if they had recently ended. Your friends were mostly women, many of whom you had met on Internet sites and "befriended"...you don't seem to have a lot of serious friendships with men. Don't you find that a little odd, Robert?

You complained every day about something that was going on in your life. I allowed you to vent and get everything off your chest and then you always hung up. Did it ever occur to you that maybe I wanted to talk about my feelings too? After our phone conversations, I remember thinking aloud, "Oh, I didn't get to tell him about...so and so. Oh well, I will tell him next time," and I would jot it down to remind myself to tell you later. After awhile, I had a list of things that I never got to tell you.

I put up with all of your faults, your crazy mood swings, the fact that you had to have things your way and your constant negativity. I overlooked and accepted things "for better or worse." But the moment you found fault with me in some way everything seemed to change. Does that not seem bizarre to you???

You talked about how clingy your ex-girlfriend was, yet you made me feel so insecure at times that I also felt clingy. Did you ever think that perhaps YOU were the reason your partners seemed clingy and insecure? Or did it not occur to you to accept blame for anything? You just went seamlessly from relationship to relationship, without looking back. You probably told all of your partners THE SAME THINGS, every one of us probably felt as if WE were "the one"...that you had FINALLY found ideal love with us. Then you just seemed to grow bored and walk away; there was no gradual fading of the relationship. You made me feel as if everything were fine (sure, we had our share of what I considered to be "normal" lows in our relationship, but I thought we were working on them. I didn't think they were reason enough to end the relationship) and then, out of the blue, you said you weren't happy and were ready to "move on!" What was that all about??? Do YOU even know?

I don't think you do. But I believe you are most likely suffering from a personality disorder called "Narcissistic Personality Disorder" (NPD). Yes, it is an actual mental disorder. You have many of the character traits of a Narcissist and I have reason to believe you have NPD based on things you have told me about your childhood and based on the way you treated me during our relationship.

PLEASE take the time to read this, Robert. I don't hate you. And hopefully I will never get to that point. Right now, I have bouts of pity for you and sometimes I still feel love in my heart for you, or for the person I thought you were, and for what I thought we had. That is because I am not disordered…not in that way, at least. I am capable of feeling empathy with others; I am not a robot.

People suffering from NPD are not capable of feeling empathy or similar emotions. Something happened to these individuals during important personality development stages and they were forced to go into a defense mode of some sort in order to protect themselves. Narcissists believe that they are not good enough as themselves so they split themselves into a real and a false self. Their false self is one they create for approval. Their false self is positive, strong, successful and adored by all. They go to great lengths to hide their "true" self, because they have formed a very negative opinion of it, based on the childhood incident that initially spurred the splitting.

This may seem ridiculous to you and more than likely, you are not going to buy into it. After all, Narcissists live in denial; they feel nothing is really wrong with them, they are the victims and no one really understands them. But take a moment to think about it. Do you remember what *you told me about your mother? Wouldn't that serve as a classic example of a traumatic childhood experience? Not all reasons for splitting can actually be identified, but I believe yours can. Because Narcissists are treated as extensions of their parents, they learn to treat their partners that way, as well.*

Robert, I hope you will seriously consider undertaking some type of therapy. Though much literature in the past has labeled NPD as incurable, psychologists agree that Narcissists can learn to identify certain confusing feelings and even understand why they are experiencing them. They can learn to react in certain ways and can even learn how to stay in long-term relationships with one partner at a time. There is help available for you. You just have to be willing to accept the fact that you need it.

Please do not think that I am saying all of this just to make you angry or to get revenge for the way you treated me. As I said before, I do not hate you. I still have moments where I feel love for you. I want to be able to reach out to you one last time in an effort to get you the help you so desperately need.

If you go online you can research it for yourself. There will be lists of NPD character traits and I am sure you will recognize some of them as your own. A Narcissist feels he will eventually find "ideal love." He is on a constant quest to find it. "Ideal love" doesn't exist, except in a Narcissist's mind. To a Narcissist, "ideal love" is a perfect love without mistakes. Once anything occurs in his relationship that isn't "perfect," the Narcissist balks and runs to his next victim.

Think about it, Robert. Didn't you do that with me...and with the woman you dated before me? As soon as the "honeymoon phase" of the relationship was over, you lost interest. Things weren't "perfect." It's possible that someone told you that you weren't the wonderful person you tried to project. Maybe your partner needed some attention for herself. For whatever reason, things weren't ideal for you anymore and you felt the need to end things. You didn't even give an indication that you felt that way and you simply left. Don't you see how that could be confusing for your partners? Don't you see how that would leave them feeling clingy and insecure as they tried to gain understanding or closure? You have to open your eyes to this.

I used to see your love for motorcycles as adventurous, but while studying NPD I learned that Narcissists are often drawn toward danger. They may race cars, ride motorcycles or have unprotected sex with multiple partners. I don't know if that is because they feel invincible due to their "omnipotence," or if they subconsciously have a death wish because of the misery they continuously suffer. Either way, I now look at all your characteristics in a different light.

I used to love the fact that you wanted to spend so much time talking on the phone with me. My friends tried to convince me that guys don't usually spend that much time talking on the phone, but I felt special that you wanted to invest that many hours getting to know me and telling me about yourself. Since then, I have learned that Narcissists don't like being alone with their "true" selves. They need constant reassurance of their "false" selves. They usually stay busy or surround themselves with people who will mirror the image they wish to project. But when they are alone with themselves, they fear coming face-to-face with their "real" selves so they will spend hours talking on the phone as their "false" personas in order to avoid that situation. I feel used looking back on those long, late-night phone calls. You didn't really care what time of the night you called me. No consideration was given to me or to the fact that I had to get up early the next morning. You were just using me in order to continue hiding from your "real" self! My own insecurities led me to believe I was the special one because I was the one you were calling. But you considered yourself to be the "special" one. I was just the one listening to you at the time. It could have been, and probably was, someone else who was listening many other times.

You might think I am being delusional. Just because I have been studying this disorder, you may feel that I am misinterpreting your behavior. But there are way too many coincidences. The fact that you moved on so quickly, without looking back...classic NPD!

Robert, when you left, I sat around trying to figure out what it was that I had done to push you away. I felt as if it had to be my fault. You had convinced me that I was the perfect mate for you, your "ideal love," so I felt I had to have done something that made you feel disgusted all of a sudden. I wracked my brain and felt myself grow more and more confused and insecure. I also longed for you and for your touch. I wanted to be with you again; I wanted things to be the way they had been at the beginning of our relationship. I missed hearing my cell phone ring all the time and missed getting cute text messages from you. I missed opening my email and seeing your name in my Inbox. I missed planning dates with you. I felt as if my life had ended...yet yours continued...without a hitch. You went right into another relationship as if I had never existed. Does that not seem strange to you? Did it never dawn on you that after spending that much time in a relationship with someone, someone to whom you had professed undying love and loyalty, that you needed to have some down time for recovery? Normal people have to grieve such losses. You simply ignored it and moved along; you wrote another script with another leading lady and lived out that fantasy with her. You didn't bother to look back once to see the damage you had left behind!!!

We are told we are not really capable of loving anyone else until we love ourselves. A Narcissist is incapable of loving his "true" self; therefore, he can never truly love anyone else. Those early feelings you mistook for love in your relationships were actually feelings of infatuation that you magnified because you wanted so badly to possess an "ideal love."

If I hadn't learned about Narcissistic Personality Disorder and convinced myself that you must be afflicted with it, I would have spent years feeling anger and disgust for you. Now I have moments of pity for you. I realize it isn't something you chose, or even something you realize you have. I feel pity because something happened to you when you were that sweet, little boy I saw in those pictures that made you feel you had to create a more loveable, acceptable version of yourself. I pity you because I see how you seem to go from relationship to relationship without ever obtaining "ideal love." I feel sorry for you because I know what you are searching for doesn't really exist and I also know that I can never convince you of this.

I've found out that narcissists have been compared to vampires, soulless creatures on an endless quest, using people as supply. They discard the people after they obtain what they need from them and continue their futile journeys. That analogy breaks my heart, Robert! I hate to think of you on that journey. I hate to think of all of the women you will destroy along the way.

Do you know what they call the partners of Narcissists? Supply. That is what I was to you, Robert...SUPPLY. You needed someone to lift you up, make you feel worthy and save you from the negatives that seemed to overwhelm you at that time. You got me, and boy, was I ever good supply! No wonder you came back for more. But after I realized the deal, I no longer wanted to be a part of it. I wanted to be someone's partner, not a tool that he used for self-satisfaction that was discarded when he felt it was no longer useful to him.

In normal relationships, partners are there to lift each other. They are there to help project the positive versions of each other. There were elements of normalcy in our relationship. According to some of the research I have done on NPD (yes, I have been lapping up all the information I can find on this subject) there are different levels of narcissism. Some Narcissists are physically violent and some are even criminals. At least you aren't a violent criminal.

I could write volumes to you on this disorder, but you probably wouldn't read it. I'm sure you don't believe that there is anything wrong with you, except for your "uncanny ability to choose the wrong partners,"— classic.

This letter isn't going to be mailed; you aren't going to read it. I know now that you wouldn't heed the advice and that you will continue going from victim to victim on your search for the non-existent "ideal love." You will continue to blame the world for your worries. You will always take other people's words, thoughts and even interests as your own. You are never going to change. BUT I AM!

I have begun to understand why I stayed with you for so long and why I allowed you to treat me the way you did. At first, I thought I was just a sweet and understanding person. I viewed myself as someone who saw the silver lining inside every cloud, someone who was going to help you realize your journey had finally ended and someone who was going to spend the rest of her days making you happy and being that "ideal woman" for you.

As I look back, I realize the man I had actually been married to was a Narcissist just as you are. I wasn't even aware of it back then. How crazy is that? I had already learned how to walk on eggshells around him so I was primed for you. For some wacky reason, I believed it was my responsibility to make other people happy. What about ME? Why did I feel the need to justify, cover and protect? Why did I allow myself to give up my own interests, my friends and even some of my family members to be able to devote more of myself to you?

Through my research of NPD I have learned that not all partners of Narcissists are as co-dependent as I was with you. There are actually varying degrees of narcissism and varying degrees of dysfunctional behavior by their partners. But I am learning about my own behavior and it is giving me strength.

In a way, you have actually been a positive force in my life, Robert. I realize that by saying this I am actually giving you narcissistic supply (yes, once again you did something life-changing for someone…all hail the mighty Narcissist). However, since I do not intend to mail this letter, you will never know that!

I am becoming educated about NPD and Narcissists. This has led me on a journey of self-discovery. Along that journey, I have discovered my own co-dependent tendencies. I now acknowledge my desire to "fix things" and make everything right. I realize now that somewhere along the way I had lost myself and my identity and had become a mirror to reflect the important people in my life. Their interests became my own as I tried to shape myself into their perfect mate or friend.

Today, I am spending my time getting closer to my daughter and trying to reconnect with myself. It hasn't been easy because I don't really know who I am. In some ways I am like you, Robert. I don't have my own identity either; I gain it from others. But the difference is that I am able to SEE that about myself and am working toward fixing it.

I know this letter won't be my cure for the pain you left behind. I am aware that I haven't completely rid myself of my co-dependency. I also know there will still be times when I'll miss you, long for your touch and want what I thought we had. But I am well on my way to recovery. While I know I will miss you, there is no way that I would ever be able to get back together with you knowing what I now know! To be in a relationship with you, I would have to compromise my integrity. I would have to look the other way when you came home late from "work." I would have to pretend not to notice when you checked out other women right in front of me. I would have to suck it up and deal with the many comparisons to your past lovers. I would have to pretend to believe you when you said you were on the Internet researching something for work. I would have to deal with the constant devaluation. In order to stay with you, I would have to start believing those negative things about myself. I would have to believe that I wasn't really worthy of your love, I couldn't really get anyone better and I should just be grateful for what I did have. When I looked at my reflection in the mirror, I would eventually see an unreliable, bitter, insecure, clingy, unworthy person staring back. Staying with you would mean complete self-destruction.

I really do hope something will happen that causes you to look within and seek professional help. I want you to be able to understand why you feel the way you do…. and learn to deal with your disorder.

But for now, I am on my own quest…one of self-discovery and healing. I want you to know that I forgive you Robert, not for you, but for myself. If I hang onto any anger or bitterness I may have for you, I will just be trading one abuse for another. I refuse to allow myself to be abused any longer.

Good luck and goodbye,

Linda

Linda's letter to Robert was therapeutic even though she knew he would never read it. As she wrote, she had bouts of self-discovery, helping her understand why she was drawn to people like Robert. So she continued with her writings. Each new letter seemed to give her more insight and emotional strength. Linda would still become slightly depressed and even miss Robert or their relationship. But her newfound awareness caused her to appreciate the fact that she was no longer in a relationship with him.

She knew mailing the letter to Robert would be useless, because he would only view it as the ranting of a woman scorned. There is no way he would see himself as someone afflicted with a personality disorder. Narcissists do not see their own shortcomings. Someone else usually causes the negatives in their lives. To Robert, Linda was just someone he met on his journey to find ideal love. At first, he thought she may have been "the one," but then he realized he was sorely mistaken because she seemed to possess many disappointing qualities that were not evident in the beginning of their relationship. When he made his exodus, Robert didn't see it as an abrupt end. He had been planning his escape for weeks, possibly even months. Linda seemed to overreact and become an insecure, clingy person. He felt as if *he* were the one who had "dodged a bullet."

This might be a good time for you to write a letter to your N. We are never given proper closure with N's due to the constant rewriting of their scripts. Sometimes this type of closure is all you can have. Trying to explain to an N that he has put you through pain would be an impossible task. Just as you are reeling from the N's grand exit, you probably will learn that he is in the honeymoon stages of another relationship. His gaslighting and accusations may make it impossible for you to gain sympathy or closure anyway. So here is an opportunity to write down your inner feelings. Write him a letter or series of letters you will never send. Tell him all about his disorder and how he used you for narcissistic supply. Explain to him how specific criticisms felt to you and how you tried so hard to believe in him. Get it all out. Vent away. This therapy will bring you nearer to closure on the unhappy relationship which demeaned you. You'll be closer to creating a new, stronger self.

Chapter 7

Know Thyself...

As you've learned, venting to your N in a letter that will never be mailed can surprisingly bring you feelings of closure...or at least semi-closure.

Like Linda who expressed her feelings to Robert in her letters, and began to examine the possibility that she had co-dependent tendencies, you too will gain insights into your own feelings and motivations; you will learn how N's seem to be drawn to co-dependents, because they have a subconscious desire to be mothered and taken care of. Narcissists also are often aware that many co-dependent types have a fear of abandonment and they use that fear to maintain control over them. They threaten to leave their partners if they don't "shape up."

If you are wondering whether or not you may have co-dependent tendencies, check out the following list of co-dependent characteristics, located on the next page.

Co-Dependency Checklist
- You base your feelings of self worth on your partner's approval.
- You try to solve your partner's problems because you feel directly affected by his/her troubles.
- Your primary goal is to satisfy and care for him/her.
- You feel happy when you are able to solve problems for your partner.
- You put aside your interests and spend time focusing on his/her hobbies.
- You feel your partner reflects you and you choose his/her clothing and have say in regards to his/her appearance.
- You view your positive qualities as what you have to offer others.
- You are unaware of what you want and are concerned with what your partner would like.
- You have dreams of your future which include your partner.
- You are careful not to provoke your partner's anger.
- You are afraid of rejection from your partner.
- You are generous with your partner in order to feel secure and prove your love in the relationship.
- As you involve yourself with your partner, you lose contact with friends and family.
- You put your own values aside in order to relate to him/her.
- You hold his/her opinion in high regard.
- The quality of your partner's life has an impact on the quality of your own life.
- Positive comments from your partner can give you an emotional high; a negative one can leave you at an extreme low.

*(BASED ON THE THEORIES OF MELODIE BEATTIE AND OUR OWN.)

How did you do? Do you possess any of those characteristics? Just because you may have co-dependent tendencies doesn't mean that you are co-dependent. Becoming aware of those tendencies allows you to work on new actions and responses. Rather than conditioned reactions, you can explore and put into place deliberate responses. There is power in gaining that type of control over yourself.

We often describe ourselves to others realistically by expressing ideas about our own personality and feelings we have gained over time. However, we sometimes take actions that contradict those descriptions. Since actions speak louder than words, our actions tell who we *really* are. Our words may tell someone that we do not like being ignored or that we expect special treatment on certain occasions, but our actions can reveal that we don't really mind being ignored or that gifts aren't necessarily that important.

When we allow ourselves to stay in abusive situations contrary to our spoken disapproval, our actions give permission for the continuation of such treatment. If we say we are sick of being treated a certain way, yet do nothing but complain about it, what our abuser hears is, "That's okay. Keep treating me that way. All I will do is complain about it or feel sorry for myself…every time you do it." If we *show*, rather than *tell*, who we are or what we will or won't tolerate, we leave no room for misinterpretation.

Exhibiting this kind of telling action is sometimes difficult for a co-dependent or a person with co-dependent tendencies, because he often doesn't know who he really is. He spends so much time mirroring the important people in his life that he tends to lose sight of his own individuality.

Being co-dependent makes it more difficult but not impossible to break away from an unhealthy relationship. Once you become aware of your own weaknesses, you can work to recognize specific patterns of behavior and avoid repeating them by adopting and instituting new responses.

Many people do not realize that while an N is attracted to co-dependent personalities, he is also a co-dependent. The N relies entirely on external validation for his sense of self-worth. He resents and even devalues supply because he realizes his dependency upon it. An N gains the good feelings he has about himself from his partner's approval. He identifies himself with his partner and focuses his attention on manipulating her. He considers his partner to be a reflection of him and his fear of rejection determines his behavior. He counts on her weaknesses and her co-dependent tendencies as a means to gain control over her.

In her self-revealing letters, Linda accused Robert of going seamlessly from relationship to relationship without looking back at any damage he may have caused. Because the N doesn't interpret his actions in the same way his partner does, his view of the situation is from a victim's standpoint. He doesn't see himself as an abuser; instead, he views himself as an unfortunate soul on an endless journey to obtain ideal love. He feels cursed by an uncanny ability to attract all the wrong women but never gives up the hope of finally "getting it right."

In fact, before Robert met Linda, he had many failed relationships. Robert felt he was just unlucky in love and had yet to meet the right person. When Linda tried to imagine Robert going from woman to woman, telling each one that she was the perfect fit or everything he had ever wanted in a woman, she saw pre-meditated manipulation and viewed Robert as a monster. N's are considered "monsters" since they are compared to vampires or soulless creatures concerned with their own well being, even at the expense of others, but not all of their actions are pre-meditated. In fact, many times the N is at the mercy of his inner demons.

N's convince themselves that they are special and they expect others to recognize this and help them maintain that status. They believe there is a perfect, ideal love out there and it is their responsibility to find it.

At the onset of each new relationship, the N believes "this could be it." When she tells her partner he is the perfect fit or the best lover she has ever had, she really believes it to be true. She wants so badly to be done with her tiresome journey and settle into "happily ever after" that she makes herself believe she has finally arrived at the destination. Her disappointing past relationships, as far back as her childhood, are what motivates her to continue her quest for ideal love.

When the victim of an N reflects upon her relationship and her partner's behavior, she tends to view him as a player, a mighty destroyer, someone who deceives to get what he wants, and then tosses people aside with no remorse as he continues to play his game. There is actually some truth in this belief, because the entire entity of the Narcissist is based on a lie. He created a false self as a means of acceptance and approval and was forced to cultivate that lie in order to maintain his existence. He pushes his true self further into his subconscious by morphing into different identities and reflecting characteristics of those around him. There is no rest for the weary N, as he must constantly "tread water" to maintain his false self.

You probably are realizing by this time that the more you learn about NPD the less time you are spending feeling sorry for the N. Sure, flashes of pity enter your mind as you realize your N feels so badly about his true self. There will be moments when you want to hold him and "make it better." Part of that is your co-dependent side wanting to fix things, but another part is your compassion for other human beings. It is always painful to watch someone suffer, even if we feel he/she deserves it. As you grow more knowledgeable about NPD, you will feel less pity for your N. While his inclinations may be on autopilot, his ability to make choices is fine. Whether it is due to weakness or a total lack of empathy, the N's choices are deliberate. No one can muster pity for someone who intentionally makes wrong choices. Keep that in mind as you continue this journey. There is a certain amount of sorrow and sympathy, which is natural, but do not let that hinder your journey of understanding and healing.

The Splitting Image…
Earlier in the book, we referred to how N's "split" themselves into a false and a true self as a defense mechanism during an important stage of personality development. By allowing us to join her journey as Linda recovers from her situation with Robert, she has revealed the dynamics of the Narcissistic relationship. Looking at Jody's relationship offers a glimpse into a situation with prime conditions for such a splitting:

Jody was five years old when her mother left home. Her father, Paul, worked as a mechanic in his own garage that never quite got off the ground. "She never thought I was good enough for her," Paul often said to his friends at night at the local pub. "She never gave me a chance to get my business going." Paul trashed the few pictures that revealed the striking resemblance between Jody and her mother one year after he had last seen Jody's mother. Jody's own memories of her mother faded each year, and as Paul could barely mutter her name without cursing, Jody's few memories of her mother became tainted with bitterness—first her father's, then her own. Eventually, the bitterness was one of the few things Jody and her father had in common—that and the fantasy he frequently shared with her of moving to California to open a hot rod shop.

Jody's father worked long hours, so he paid his neighbor Debbie to watch Jody until she was old enough to go to school. The dream of moving to California became Jody's personal fantasy, though her father drank more and spoke less and less about it as time passed. If asked as she grew up about her early childhood,

Jody would reference the fact that her mother left her when she was just a small kid. She went to work when she was sixteen, and later obtained her GED.

Jody's pregnancy was not planned. Needless to say, her dream of going to California was postponed when Brandon was born. Brandon's father was nowhere to be found, and Jody's father was barely able to make ends meet and could offer no financial help. He was drinking again and Jody was alone. She desperately struggled to pay the bills while trying to raise a child, and was under a great deal of stress. One of the few things that sustained her was the dream that she would someday go to California, and that Brandon—who was "exceptionally beautiful"—would become a famous movie star and make them rich. When Brandon was first born and she felt overwhelmed, she would pick the baby up and rock him while reciting the story of her California fantasy.

Jody soon noticed that often she could not console Brandon when he cried, which she found very frustrating. She decided that when Brandon cried he needed to stay in his crib, which also allowed her to get things done. Her life was very difficult as a single mother. As time went on, she learned to ignore Brandon's crying, and thought she had read somewhere that it was good for babies to cry. Many times Brandon cried himself to sleep, and the resulting peace and quiet was like paradise for Jody. Sometimes Jody wondered if she were a good mother, and then concluded that at least she was better than HER mother had been.

However, when Jody rocked Brandon and talked about moving to California, Brandon did not cry. Jody felt a special mother-son bond was forming. When Brandon seemed cranky or was asking for attention, he was put in the crib. When Jody felt lonely and hopeless and trapped, she rocked Brandon. During those times, Brandon instinctively responded to his mother's nourishing, life-giving attention by smiling and cooing, and he quickly learned that crying would land him in the crib. In essence, Jody did not respond to Brandon's emotions and needs just as her mother had not responded to Jody's emotional needs.

Nevertheless, Jody grew more attached to Brandon, and she began to see him as an important part of her future.

Because his mother did not often comfort Brandon when he cried, he felt abandoned and alone many times during his childhood. His need for nurturing in general was often ignored, and the anxiety and emptiness he felt was more than he could bear. Brandon became desperate in his need to have his mother acknowledge his most basic feelings and comfort him. Jody, preoccupied with her own needs, relied heavily on her parenting technique of ignoring and separating when Brandon became "whiny" or "difficult."

Finally, as a reaction to the repeated emotional neglect, a part of Brandon "shut down" in much the same way that one goes into shock after a trauma. It could be said that the normal stages of child development were interrupted. Brandon was not truly able to trust that the most significant person in his universe recognized him, his feelings, his needs… everything that is a young child's existence. Without this basic trust in his most significant other, Brandon's very identity and sense of self would be scarred. The only other significant person left in his universe was himself, so Brandon retreated inward, thwarted in his attempt to "attach" to his mother in any real way.

Brandon's retreat inward could be seen as the first step in "splitting" his identity. This was not just a child becoming more resilient and emotionally self-reliant; it was not a way to cope with feelings of neglect by somehow comforting himself. Those skills do not emerge until a later stage of development. This change required that Brandon deny his true feelings altogether and that he place himself at the center of his universe, where existing alone he could develop ideal, grandiose, and magical fantasies that moved him away from the pain of his emotional neglect, and ever closer to an ideal image of himself. Brandon grew numb to his painful feelings of rejection in much the same way a neglected child in an orphanage eventually stops crying. It could be said that Brandon's reaction to his trauma essentially re-constructed his personality at that point, and the effects of this splitting would haunt him his entire life.

Another important factor in Brandon's environment shaped his personality development profoundly: he learned that by focusing more and more on his mother's feelings he was able to receive a special type of attention, for in this relationship of mother and son, the emotional needs of the mother were more important than the emotional needs of the child. His own true feelings now seemed unfamiliar and even strange to him, and his "true self" became more distant and foreign. Since the expression of Brandon's "true self" had frequently led to removal from his mother and placement in the crib, and later his room, a new sense of self began to form. This "false self" formed around Brandon's grandiose and magical world in which he was the center. In time, Brandon's "false self" became powerful and altered its form in order to receive attention and adoration from his mother.

Brandon formed a special identity—an identity that would reinforce his grand and powerful position as the center of his universe. He discovered vast reserves of attention and acceptance from his mother at certain times. That acceptance began at an early age when his mother rocked him and talked about their future together in California. From the time that he could understand them, Brandon heard messages that he was special, and that he was going to make them both rich and famous someday. Brandon's sense of happiness, his fulfillment and his very identity, were groomed and shaped by his mother. In this family there was no place for feelings that were authentic and true. As a result, Brandon learned to live his life according to his "false self."

Yet deep inside, in places he could not visit, Brandon's primitive fears and anger haunted him. These feelings were threatening and intolerable, for they were the dying cries of his true self. Brandon's true self had been rejected, however, and it now represented everything in him that was negative. Brandon's only effective coping mechanism was to re-affirm his position as the center of his universe by inflating his grandiose fantasies and denying his negative identity. Anytime Brandon felt threatened, he relied on this method of defense.

Brandon learned to entertain himself and was in many ways self-suffi-cient. He did not seem to enjoy playing with other children in the neighborhood, and frequently got angry when he did. When he was five, the game Brandon most liked playing was "Hollywood" with his mother. In this masquerade, Jody dressed Brandon up like a movie star and took pictures of him. She talked about the family dream of moving to California, and that she was going to make it happen for him no matter what. She gave him "pretend roles" to play and tried to build Brandon's self-esteem by assuring him that he would be a movie star someday, and that nothing could hold him back.

Jody became so entangled in Brandon's identity that she would often make Brandon feel guilty if he behaved in a way that triggered her fear of loneliness, or if his own true needs tried to emerge and take control. At these times, Jody often talked about the financial difficulties the two of them faced, and the fact that she had worked hard all her life to provide for Brandon, and she never failed to bring up her dream of their going to California. After all, a loving mother only wants what's best for her son, and she never wants him to forget how special he is.

Brandon's situation is only one of many possible incidents that could instigate the splitting process for an N. The mother of an N is con-sidered to have an enormous influence on his splitting, but it isn't always a caregiver that influences the splitting process, nor is it always a male that experiences it.

Chapter 8

Female Narcissists...

While it is generally agreed that seventy-five percent of individuals afflicted with NPD are male, there is no shortage of female N's. Female N's are shaped in the same way as male N's. In some cases, female N's are merely extensions of the narcissistic parent who raised them; they continue reflecting that parent throughout adulthood. Other women become afflicted with NPD after traumatic childhood experiences that may have caused them to "split" their personalities, therefore becoming the adults they were *expected to be*.

Narcissistic mothers have tremendous expectations for their children. Nothing ever seems to meet the standards of a narcissistic mother. Because a mother with NPD considers her children to be mere *extensions of herself*, when anyone compliments *her children* the mother feels the need to express modesty and occasionally devalues the compliment. For example, if someone were to tell a narcissistic mother who has a child with a weight problem that her child is pretty, she may respond by saying something like, "Pretty fat, maybe." An N mother wouldn't be able to accept the compliment because of the feelings she has about her true self. A compliment about her children would translate as a direct compliment about the narcissistic mother and her negative self image would take over. The mother would feel as if she should express modesty or "jokingly" devalue the compliment in order to feel comfortable about accepting praise from someone who obviously didn't know the real "truth" about her. Children of narcissistic mothers may misinterpret this behavior as insults directed toward *them* and spend their lives trying to be good enough to gain approval from their mothers.

Just as there are varying degrees of narcissism within males afflicted with NPD, the same is true with females. Some mothers afflicted with NPD often feel as if their daughters are their rivals. Narcissistic mothers have even been known to feel jealous of attention given to their daughters by their daughters' fathers. Victims of narcissistic mothers have recounted memories of their childhoods where their mothers had actually accused them of trying to *seduce* their fathers. Jenny, a victim with whom we spoke, recalled a devastating time when her mother abandoned her and her father. The N mother called over her shoulder as she walked out the door, "Now you two can have each other!"

Some N's have extreme degrees of paranoia, such as N mothers who become jealous of the attention a father may give to his daughter or N fathers who use extreme measures to tear down their daughters while praising their sons; the majority of those afflicted with NPD, however, seem to fall somewhere in the middle of those extreme degrees.

Ask yourself if you recognize any of the traits described in the following case study of an N female's everyday existence:

Beverly is a middle-aged woman with four children whose ages range from seven to nineteen. When she was in school, Beverly had participated in a few extra-curricular activities, but her parents had been too busy to go to her games

*or to watch her theatrical performances. Beverly had felt the sting of embarrass-
ment each time she was one of the only students whose parent was absent on
parent night. When she was congratulated, it was always by a friend's parent,
instead of her own, after a school production. Because of her own feeling of dep-
rivation of lack of parental attention, Beverly had promised herself that she
would be involved with every aspect of her children's lives when she had her own
family. And she was, in a sense, re-living her own childhood through her children. Not a game or practice occurred without Beverly sitting on the sidelines
cheering and critiquing her children. Since Beverly felt she needed to be several
places, sometimes at once, this made things quite hectic around her household.
She was always in a rush...hurrying off to one event after another. Screaming
matches would often precede each new jaunt as she piled everyone into the family's van and drove to different destinations.*

*Beverly had learned to comfort herself with food at an early age and had
also passed that defense mechanism onto her children. Doughnuts, cookies, and
chips were staple food items in her household and everyone helped himself/her-
self to these snack foods between meals. More food was consumed if there
seemed to be a stressful situation occurring at the time. Because of this, Beverly's
weight yo-yoed, which added to the low self-esteem she had developed during her
childhood.*

*The relationship between Beverly and her husband was a neurotic one.
Ted, Beverly's husband, had been raised by a very controlling narcissistic mother
and had spent his childhood trying to measure up to her continuously rising
standards. Ted had been shaped into a classic co-dependent before he graduated
from high school so when he met Beverly in college he was primed and ready for
her to take the place of his deceased, narcissistic mother. Ted had learned at an
early age how to appease his mother and comfort her during her narcissistic
rages. He prided himself on being one of the few family members able to calm
his mother and actually bring her pleasure. However, Ted soon learned that he
was only a bandage for his mother and not a cure, for each new day brought a*

new tragedy and a new opportunity for which Ted could rush to the rescue.

Beverly kept him in prime co-dependent condition in the early years of their marriage, needing Ted to calm her down during her fits of anger. There were times when Beverly ranted for hours about remarks someone made in passing, making much more out of the comment than Ted often felt had been intended. For example, one day Beverly had run into Gail, a former classmate, who had asked about Beverly's ex-boyfriend, Scott. When Beverly told her that she and Scott had been history for several years and that she was now happily married to Ted, the classmate said, "Oh good. You were too good for Scott, anyway. I dated Scott once myself and he cheated on me!" Rather than taking the comment as a compliment, Beverly felt it was a way of insulting her and struck out at Gail. Beverly replied, "Well, Scott never cheated on me. He adored me. He just couldn't get enough of me. I only broke up with him because he was too smothering." When Beverly got home she sought out her husband and ranted about how her ex-classmate had tried to make her look bad. Ted had learned better than to disagree with Beverly's interpretation of any situation, so even though he believed that the classmate had only been trying to pay Beverly a compliment, Ted went along with Beverly's ranting and calmly tried to cheer her up. Ted even praised Beverly for "showing that classmate at thing or two."

Let's analyze the situation. Beverly's low self-esteem would not allow her to interpret her former classmate's comment as a compliment. Rather than seeing Gail's comments as an expression of "sisterhood," two young women praising themselves for having dodged the same bullet, Beverly had seen it as a slam. She saw it as a type of failure on her part. Beverly judged the remark as someone *else* pointing out something she hadn't done right or as someone *else* (Scott) who hadn't been able to love the "real" Beverly. In truth, Scott had shown Beverly disrespect when they were together and that was still an issue for her so Beverly had to devalue her former classmate in order to gain back some of the control she felt she had lost and then lost again when the classmate had "insulted" her.

Beverly continued to rage over the situation to her husband, because devaluing her classmate hadn't been enough to convince Beverly's "true" self of the classmate's intentions. To believe that her former classmate had meant no harm, Beverly would have to admit that something was wrong with *herself* for feeling so defensive about an innocent comment. She had worked too hard to convince herself and others that she was nothing like the "true" self she had so carefully hidden. Sometimes an N needs a lot of encouragement and lots of bandages to finally be convinced of his/her "false" self.

This is why co-dependent relationships are so sought by N's. Co-dependents have been trained and conditioned to encourage. Ted had spent his life encouraging his mother and had gained his own self-worth from those victories. Each time Beverly had such a crisis (and there were many) Ted was able to convince her that she had done the right thing by reacting as she had. When Beverly would calm down and get in a better mood, Ted's own self-worth was raised a notch. Ted had long since learned to never disagree with Beverly if he wanted to keep peace in the household. Beverly could make everyone's life miserable if she was thwarted. As a middle-aged man, Ted developed a heart condition in large measure due to stress. However, Ted's outward calm compliance was belied by his own inner turmoil.

Holidays can be very stressful for individuals afflicted with NPD. This is usually because the holidays focus on things not directly related to the N. The N needs to feel special at all times and cannot stand sharing the spotlight of attention. He expects to receive gifts that express how others feel about him/her. The N takes inexpensive or unplanned gifts as an insult. Sometimes an N will appreciate a gift he/she has received until he/she sees a better gift received by someone else. It then becomes a competition of sorts.

An illustration of how holidays can be disastrous for those

involved with N's came about when Beverly was chosen to host the annual family Christmas dinner at her house.

Beverly's entire household was upset and apprehensive as everyone received orders to help clean and organize. N's are usually good at delegating authority and Beverly had seen to it that every member of her family had a time consuming task to complete. Stress and tension built up. Finally, when the guests began arriving, Beverly, her husband and children were exhausted and not in festive moods.

But they tried to relax as family members began to exchange light banter at the dinner table. Everyone laughed at each other's jokes and Beverly's brother complimented Ted's casserole. Just when things appeared to be going better, one of the guests, Beverly's brother, made a comment that was perfectly innocent to him, but caused the guests to stare at each other with foreboding. They knew Beverly would take the comment negatively, even though their uncle had a sparkle in his eye when he said it. Beverly's husband and children were especially upset. They knew when the guests would leave Beverly would show the narcissistic rage she was keeping undercover.

Sure enough, after the guests had left, Beverly began throwing plates in the sink and ranting about the comment. Ted had enjoyed himself and had felt good about the way everyone had seemed to enjoy his casserole. He wasn't in the mood to hear another one of Beverly's tirades. So he made the mistake of suggesting that perhaps she had misinterpreted the comment. That is when Beverly lit into Ted. How dare Ted take sides with her brother over her? Did Ted not know the negative comments her brother had said about him over the years? Beverly insisted that nobody knew the devious workings of her brother's mind the way she did. Sure, he could come across innocent to the untrained eye, but he had evil intentions and she recognized them because she had grown up with him.

On this occasion, Ted stuck to his belief that Beverly's brother had made an innocent comment and that it hadn't caused harm. The dinner went well. Ted insisted and commented on how comfortable everyone had seemed (in spite

*of the fact that Beverly usually made people feel uncomfortable in her house),
and how Beverly's brother had seemed relaxed and casual when he had made the
comment. Ted was tired of always giving in to Beverly and agreeing with her
distorted ideas just to keep the peace. He was tired of feeling like less of a man
because he allowed his wife to run the show. It was time to put his foot down
and stand up for something he actually believed in. Beverly was livid. The fact
that someone could disagree with her seemed absurd. She flew into a rage that
topped any Ted had seen. She began criticizing him and acted disgusted with
him. "The only reason you are sticking up for my brother is because he bragged
about your nasty casserole. You were so proud of that stupid casserole! How do
you think they would feel if they knew it was from a box? Homemade, my eye!
If they only knew what a phony you were, they wouldn't spend any time brag-
ging on your pre-made foods. Now that I think about it, I am starting to wonder if you don't have a thing for my brother. I noticed how you kept staring at
him at dinner and laughing at all of his dumb jokes. I know others had to be
aware of it also, because it was so very obvious. Is that what it is? Could it be
that you have latent homosexual tendencies and are attracted to my brother?
That's it, isn't it? Well, well, well…I seemed to have hit the nail on the gay head!"*

*Ted was devastated. He had no idea that Beverly could be so cruel. He
stopped drying the dishes and went upstairs, half expecting Beverly to follow
and apologize for being so mean. She never came. She slept in another room that
night. Several days following the incident, neither one of them spoke to each
other. Finally, Ted couldn't take the silent treatment any longer. Besides, he did-
n't like the way Beverly seemed to be taking it out on the kids. Also, Beverly
seemed to get in little digs about Ted every chance she got…even to their children. Longing for peace, Ted felt miserable, so he went to Beverly and apologized. He knew an apology wouldn't be enough so he also made negative
comments about her brother to make Beverly laugh. Once he had lightened her
mood he offered to take her out to dinner that night. Things were back to
"normal" once again.*

Upon analyzing Beverly's actions, we can see that because she felt threatened, she became very defensive. N's need to feel right at all times. When people disagree with them, Narcissists don't see those disagreements as other opinions; they see them as direct attacks against their integrity. Since Ted refused to side with Beverly even after she began her angry tirade, Beverly felt the need to devalue Ted in order to gain back some of the control she felt she was losing. To Beverly, Ted seemed to be getting too confident and needed to be taken down a notch or two. By attacking his sexuality and accusing Ted of having latent homosexual feelings for her brother, Beverly was able to catch him off guard and make him feel miserable at the same time. When the other guests bragged about Ted's casserole, Beverly felt annoyed that her even greater accomplishments to make the evening a success weren't paramount. Beverly felt threatened because *someone else* (even though it was her own spouse) received more attention than she. That is why she felt the need to devalue the casserole.

Part of the reason Ted was so proud that everyone enjoyed his casserole was because he wanted Beverly to be proud of him. Co-dependents need constant approval from their partners. When Beverly devalued Ted's casserole she knew he would be devastated, because not only was she showing disapproval, but also disgust.

Another part of the reason Ted wanted Beverly to forgive him when she was the one who insulted and treated him cruelly was that co-dependents subconsciously *expect* that type of treatment. It is part of the twisted dance between an N and his/her co-dependent. Beverly's pride would not allow her to go to Ted and apologize. N's justify their cruel actions, convincing themselves that they are brought about by the misconduct of others. In her mind, Ted had intentionally refused to see the truth about Beverly's brother and had insisted upon glorifying his own petty accomplishments; in this case, the casserole. Beverly saw that as a weakness. N's are disgusted by weakness and are drawn to partners for their strength, success in certain areas, and/or beauty. They set about finding other areas to attack.

Because they have low self-esteem, N's may still feel threatened by attractive people even if they aren't somatic. This can cause even more stress for those involved with an N. *Beverly had a problem with her weight due to her habit of stress eating. Even though she was attractive, Beverly saw herself as grotesque, especially when she had gained several pounds. One summer a few months after they were married, Ted's sister, Lisa, and her husband, Harry, invited Ted and Beverly to spend a week with them at their beach house. Not realizing this would cause stress for Ted and Beverly, Lisa began looking forward to the visit. She had never had a chance to spend any quality time with Beverly and was looking forward to getting to know her new sister-in-law.*

Meanwhile, Beverly was stressing over what bathing suit to wear and complaining that every suit she owned made her look like a beached whale. Ted was spending a lot of time and energy trying to convince Beverly that she looked fine. He knew that if he didn't attempt to make Beverly feel better, she would work herself into a frenzy and cancel the trip. Ted had been looking forward to a trip to the beach because Harry had promised Ted a ride on his new boat. Ted knew he would have to buy Beverly a new wardrobe in order to convince her to go to the beach. Finally, after several new outfits and a new set of luggage, the couple were on their way to Florida. The trip down was unusually quiet. Ted only had to tell Beverly not to worry a few times. She slept most of the way.

When they arrived, Lisa ran out to meet them wearing a pair of shorts and a bikini top. Her body was in good shape and it was obvious she was no stranger to exercise as her muscles were well defined. Beverly automatically tensed and her mood dropped when she saw Lisa. Since this was early on in their marriage, Ted hadn't learned to pick up on these signals and was oblivious to Beverly's insecurities.

Later that afternoon, Ted and Beverly went back to the beach house to shower and get ready for dinner. Beverly's mood was dark and Ted made the mistake of asking her what was wrong. "Your sister, that's what's wrong," she answered. Ted was confused. He thought they had been having a good time on the beach together. Beverly hadn't seemed upset about anything and he had even seen her laughing with Lisa as they looked for seashells. "What do you mean, 'my sister'?" Ted asked.

"I just never realized how arrogant she is," Beverly replied.

"What do you mean by that?" Ted asked.

"Well, she seems to just love flaunting her body and she tried to make me feel fat and ugly all morning," Beverly complained.

"What? That doesn't sound like Lisa. She seems to really like you," Ted defended.

"I knew you would take her side. Big sister could never do anything wrong! You didn't see how she would purposely run up to me and walk beside me on the beach. She wanted her body to look good so she thought if she walked next to a fat person that she would look even better. I didn't fall for her tricks, though. I saw right through her little act. She kept sauntering around and showing off for everyone that walked by. It made me sick! I really feel sorry for Harry, bless his heart. That Jezebel is going to destroy him one day." Beverly was growing more angry and excited as she readied herself for dinner. Ted was confused. He had never seen that side of his sister, yet his new bride had picked up on it, right away. Could he have been blind to his sister's arrogance? Surely Beverly had been mistaken. When he tried to defend his sister a second time, Ted experienced Beverly's narcissistic rage. Soon Beverly began stuffing herself with food to ease the distress she felt. They had to leave early, because she said she had suddenly become ill and needed to go home.

Had Ted known about NPD he would have understood Beverly's insecurities and realized that trying to reason with her was futile.

Instead, he spent the next three weeks hearing about his "loose sister" and all the possible reasons she had turned out the way she did. Anytime Ted tried to interject a defensive comment, Beverly would include him among his other dysfunctional family members. Finally, he remained quiet. That was the beginning of insight for Ted that he needed to appease his wife when she "got in one of her moods," and since he had learned how to do that with his mother, Ted now utilized the same technique with his wife. Soon he was an expert at lifting Beverly's spirits when she became *overly sensitive*. He told himself that she was a good person. She just *took things the wrong way sometimes* and needed his wisdom and insight to set things straight.

Co-dependents need to feel as if they are special. Ted felt as if he alone understood Beverly. Because of that, Ted gained self-esteem each time he was able to change her bad mood to a more upbeat one during one of her "misunderstandings." Beverly was equally dependent upon Ted. He gave her enormous narcissistic supply (NS) and helped keep her "false self" alive. However, in reality, NS is easily replaced.

When an N sees glimpses of his/her true self, he/she feels threatened and uses rage or devaluation as ways to regain feelings of control. If those attempts don't work, an N may slip into depression. This period can also be very stressful for those involved with N's. At times, an N will *pretend* to be down in order to manipulate those around him/her. But when an N actually experiences depression, it is usually a sign of being out of control. The N will feel his/her false world crumbling...or see glimpses of his/her true self (the self he or she has tried so desperately to eliminate) and will become overwhelmed with *reality*. The N's reality is self-created and comfortable as long as there are others willing to keep it alive. To the N, losing that reality is like losing his/her mind. It can be very scary.

Sometimes, when this happens, the N may go to bed for several days. The N's family will try to lift his/her spirits in the usual conditioned ways, but once depression sets in, it becomes more difficult to change an N's mood and end his/her gloom. The family members of an N suffer right along with the N during these periods of depression. Because the N seems fragile during his/her depressed state, no one wants to cause him/her further stress. Guilt and prior conditioning cause the family members to tread very carefully in order to prevent causing more pain and anguish for the N. The partners of an N and also the children in the family (even while quite young) learn to hide their own feelings and instead respond to the mood and whims of their loved one. Co-dependent responses are formed at an early age and such responses continue in later relationships.

Chapter 9

The Angry State

One of the most defining characteristics of the N is rage. Those who have been on the receiving end of this rage know that it is unlike any other type of anger; it is unpredictable, highly over-reactive, irrational and not selective. Anyone who happens to be in the presence of a raging N is at risk for insult or attack, regardless of his/her "guilt" or "innocence." It is important to realize that the N's anger is not rationally connected to his/her experience with others. It is merely a product of his/her distorted inner world. N rage is not an attempt to resolve conflict, and it is not an expression of hurt, frustration, or any other feelings that are usually experienced in a "normal" relationship. The only goal of N rage is to *obliterate the target*. In the last chapter, Beverly and Ted's story demonstrated how Beverly ruthlessly attacked Ted each time he refused to agree with her.

As we saw with Beverly, the N expresses rage without discrimination or moderation, so the individual who somehow triggers the rage of the N will likely, regardless of the severity of his/her "transgression," become a victim of a vicious attack that is extreme. Since the N follows no ethical guidelines, he/she does not know how to fight fairly. Victims of N's have learned the hard way that any of their weaknesses or vulnerabilities could be *fair game* for attack. It is emotionally dangerous for a partner or child to be exposed to the poison of an N's rage, especially over time. Since it is not rationally connected to anything the victim said or did, it is difficult to make sense of an N's anger. The confusion of the victim is a critical strand in the web the N spins to trap the unaware and vulnerable. The N is a master at manipulation and knows the methods to use in order to effectively convince his/her victims that it was "their fault" and that the N's narcissistic rage was justified. This type of "gaslighting" is not always deliberate as the N becomes so involved with false reality that he or she often believes the carefully constructed web of lies.

Another destructive aspect of N rage is its duration. Although it is explosive and sudden, it is not so easily quenched. Because the N's rage is not rationally connected to others, it continues to seethe and burn until his internal stability is regained. N rage can be triggered when the N feels challenged, insulted or criticized—even when someone just disagrees with him. He experiences this challenge as a threat to his very identity: his false self, and the false reality he's so painstakingly created in all relationships. Because the N cannot tolerate the threat of being "unmasked" (this attack on his psychic equilibrium), his reaction is to respond aggressively, without reason and without empathy until he feels assured that his false reality is no longer threatened. This explains why narcissistic anger is not just a flash fire that quickly burns out. N's are grudge-holders and will brood for years over what others consider being trivial matters.

In order to stop the chaos and turmoil of their relationship, victims of N rage may admit to faults that aren't their own, they may beg forgiveness and they may try to make amends. However, the N still sees the person who triggered his/her rage as someone who has the potential to threaten the false self the N has so carefully fashioned. So the nature of the N rage is to attack, denigrate, and injure the "opponent" in an attempt to render him/her powerless. Co-dependents often feel obligated to accept responsibility for the irrational rages of their Narcissistic partners in order to maintain peace.

In their everyday existence, N's basically live in an ongoing state of anger (although this is usually carefully disguised and hidden beneath the surface until a rage episode). The N lives a tragic and destructive life, trying to balance on the sharp and rocky peak of his/her false self. This provides the N with feelings of grandiosity, entitlement and inflated self-importance. Much of the N's psychic energy is directed toward maintaining that balance within himself/herself and his/her environment, and the resulting stress and frustration accumulates. N's resent any force that threatens to knock them from their precarious positions "on top of the mountain." For example, N's are often very envious of others. Many feel that they must have the best of everything, or that they are in some way better than others. So when N's see others possessing special talents, landing better jobs, or buying better homes, their grandiose view is threatened by these actualities and events; they cause them to feel envious and to resent the challenges to maintaining their make-believe world in which *they* are the center of the universe. This was evident in the incident in the previous chapter when Beverly felt threatened by Lisa's body.

Many mental health professionals feel the maladaptive, destructive behavior of the N is an attempt to maintain his/her false reality in the same way that an alcoholic is desperate to construct his/her life to perpetuate his/her drinking, no matter what the cost. The false reality of an N has also been compared to the politics of a cult leader, where those who would become his/her followers must adhere to the rules and beliefs of the cult, or be cast out. To the N, out-casting is one of the worst forms of punishment he/she can give to his/her victim, because the N views his "false" self as grandiose. Therefore, becoming disconnected from the Narcissist would be a "great loss to anyone." At times, an N will disconnect himself/herself from the lives of those around him/her in order to "teach them a lesson." When he/she feels these individuals have "learned their lesson," the N may reconnect with those persons upon the understanding that the N will be treated *more carefully*. The underlying implication is if this condition is not met, the disconnection will become more permanent.

Though anger is a major part of the N's inner turmoil, he/she must find ways to disguise it so he/she can ensure an ongoing source of supply. After an N rage, N's may masterfully manipulate their victims with insincere apologies, flattery (idealization), promises to seek counseling, and false affection. Between rages, N's may act out their anger with an arsenal of subtly cruel and abusive behavior...part of the daily repertoire of their social interactions. When Beverly was upset with Ted she would insult him in front of their children. It is not unusual between rages for an N to insult or humiliate his/her partner in social settings in order to gain a sense of false control.

Many believe that the number of *females* afflicted with the disorder may be considerably higher than the reported thirty percent, because women N's tend to fall under other societal labels. For example, women who seem to manipulate or use men for personal gain are often considered to be "spoiled" or "gold diggers." Because of society's expectations or stereotyping, female N's are often overlooked.

Female N's are masters of mind games. *Narcissism* is defined as "self-love; excessive interest in one's own appearance, comfort, importance, abilities..." An N will go out of his/her way in order to ensure self-gratification. What often appear to be mind games to us are merely new scripts for the N. When things aren't going the way the N intends, he/she simply *rewrites* the script. The N needs to maintain a sense of control in his/her relationship, so when things aren't going the way the N intends, a rewrite is necessary.

Female N's tend to act out in characteristic ways. For instance, Claire was very upset about a sudden change of plans and was ranting about the new turn of events. She complained about the circumstance for hours and nothing her partner Randy did seemed to calm her. Later, someone called Claire and based on that phone conversation, she assumed Randy had talked to the caller prior to the phone call, therefore betraying her confidence. Randy tried to convince his N that the phone conversation was a coincidence and that he hadn't mentioned anything she had said to anyone. Claire said something like, "I was starting to feel close enough to you to trust you with things. I suppose now I will just have to talk to so-and-so about my personal matters." N's often *remove themselves* from people's lives as a form of punishment. N's have been known to break contact with family members and friends. They may say something such as, "We are no longer related. I hereby disconnect myself from you. If I see you on the streets, I will be decent and wave to you like I would to *any stranger*, but I no longer consider you family." While it is ludicrous to most people to become "unrelated," an N sees nothing unusual about it. After all, he/she is in charge of his/her "false" self and the script that goes along with it. If he/she no longer wants to be related to someone, a simple rewrite of the script is all that is necessary. It is extremely simple.

Not all "removals" are that drastic. Some "removals" occur, as in Claire's scenario, when the N threatened to use someone else as a confidant. N's assume that people feel privileged to have their trust. They don't confide in just *anyone*, so when Narcissists "open up" to *special* individuals they assume those individuals understand the *honorable* position they have been given. To maintain control over the entrusted individual, the N threatens to remove his/her trust and give it to someone more *worthy*. Co-dependents don't always recognize this behavior as manipulation and often unwittingly play along. People with co-dependent tendencies fear abandonment on any level; N's sense this and use it as a way to obtain narcissistic supply.

Some narcissistic head games may be cleverly disguised. Others are blatantly obvious. For example, if your N had told you to bring home milk after work one evening and you forgot, the scene may have played out something like this: Your N, upon looking out the window, noticed you were walking into the house without the milk. She ran to the door, flinging it open excitedly and said something like, "I am so glad you are home! I have been craving chocolate milk all evening!" When she "realized" you had forgotten the milk, your Narcissist feigned exaggerated disappointment. You felt horrible, especially after seeing how disappointed your N was and you even offered to go back out for milk. "No. That's okay." She said, "I will be okay until tomorrow." By not getting her way and excusing you from the task, your N got to play martyr; this allowed her to obtain double narcissistic supply.

You may have picked up on the mind games N's play when your N suddenly *came down with a headache* or when her stomach began *giving her trouble* shortly after something occurred that was out of her control. Many times N's "become ill" due to what others assume are stressful situations for the N's. What is really happening is the N is reeling out of control for whatever reason and "becoming ill" is the only way he/she can resume "control." The irony of those illnesses is that N's tend to scoff at illness in others and view them as forms of weakness; they expect others to ignore their own illnesses and press on during those times. However, when an N *really* becomes ill everyone connected to him or her must stop and take notice. N's expect people to pay special attention to them when *they* become sick. Even though an N may pretend to not want any help while he/she recovers. The truth is shown by the way he/she reacts to such neglect. An N makes it painfully obvious that he/she wants special attention during his/her illness...even if it is to be admired for his/her bravery for "not wanting attention."

Somatic female N's use their bodies to obtain narcissistic supply. They usually keep themselves well groomed and in good physical shape. They appreciate the approval they receive, but more than this, they also expect it. Some Somatic female Narcissists dress seductively in order to gain attention. Others need countless compliments...after all, they worked hard to maintain their bodies and they expect appreciation for the hard work.

When your N gave you a gift, did she/he expect you to thank her/him many times for the gift? Did you ever notice that she/he never showed the same appreciation for gifts received from you? When an N gives a gift, you can bet there is something in it for her/him. An N will be the first to tell people about the money she/he spent on someone. N's feel the need to come across as altruistic people with generous hearts. They will often invite the local newspaper to "catch them" in charity acts. It is never about the person or affiliation receiving the gift, but about the N herself/himself.

In addition to Somatic N's using their bodies to obtain narcissistic supply, they are also known to play head games. Men often overlook or are unaware of these manipulations and head games by beautiful women, calling the women "high maintenance." Unattractive manipulative females sometimes are given less-endearing labels. Either way, because of society's tendency to stereotype and label, female N's aren't always easily recognized.

Keep in mind that we all have *some* narcissistic tendencies, but that doesn't mean we have Narcissistic Personality Disorder. Narcissistic tendencies are used as defense mechanisms, and to a small degree, can be healthy. When people become mere objects with which to gain narcissistic supply, those *tendencies* are no longer healthy. As we discussed in earlier sections of this book, N's aren't always aware of the turmoil they cause in the lives of others. Some Narcissists are so involved with their scripts and their "false" selves that they don't see beyond their self-created worlds. Therefore, they really are oblivious to the feelings of others. Other Ns' seem to notice that they are causing pain in people's lives, but see those individuals as "casualties of war." N's *expect* sacrifices to be made in order to maintain their "false" selves. An N feels that most people, since they are neither special nor extraordinary, should gladly lay down their menial lives in order to preserve the life of the important N.

Have you ever noticed a time when your N seemed to become ill when other members of the family were sick? Attention given to others is stressful for the Narcissist. If family members (even the N's children) become ill, chances are the N will be lying in bed with a heating pad or tissue box. To the N the sickness is real. The stressful feelings of losing the spotlight while the children receive special attention can cause the N to experience real feelings of pain. If he/she doesn't come down with a sickness when his/her family members become ill, the Narcissist may show disgust for the family members for showing their weakness and expect them to quickly recover and get back to business as usual.

An N always seems to be thinking and planning...his/her mind never rests. It takes a lot of work to maintain control of his/her world and all the relationships involved. There never seems to be real happiness or peace for the N. Many Narcissists fear death because it symbolizes the unknown; an N realizes he/she won't have the same sense of false control in the afterlife. But what if the N convinces himself/herself that there is no afterlife? The idea of no longer existing is a devastating blow to one whose being centers on his/her own existence.

Older N's often become depressed and concerned with aging.

Somatic N's recognize their fleeting youth and realize they are no longer getting second glances from members of the opposite sex. This causes anxiety for the N as he/she begins to feel less valuable. After all, a Somatic N uses his/her body to extract narcissistic supply. There is fear in the possibility of losing the very tool used to obtain that important commodity.

One of the biggest downfalls for the N is the belief that he/she is in control. Because the N is the center of his self-created world, he feels a certain amount of pressure to maintain that world. He uses his sense of power to control those around him and to change situations in his favor. He lies awake at night creating possible scenarios for situations that may never come into existence and prides himself on all the back-up plans he invents for "just in case." Instead of viewing those situations as unnecessary worry when things *don't* play out the way he imagined, the N feels proud that, at least, he had been *prepared*.

When someone tries to convince the N of something that doesn't comply with the "false" self he/she has created, the N may project characteristics of his "real" self onto that person. For example, if a person were to call the N on some remarks he/she had made, but was now denying, the N, instead of backing down and admitting his/her wrong, the N might say, "You are a liar! You have always been a liar! Nothing you ever say is true. You have spent your entire life lying and I can never believe a word that comes out of your mouth!" This sort of attack throws the victim off track and causes him/her to become defensive in order to prove his/her honesty. Meanwhile, the heat is off the N and he/she is able to regain "control." This type of projection is a common defense mechanism for the N. After the victim has gone off to "lick his/her wounds," the N is able to continue his script, which may suddenly switch to a peaceful scene. This explains how an N can switch from a narcissistic rage to a jovial mood in a matter of minutes. The rage experienced by an N isn't emotion-induced. It is usually a defense mechanism that is no longer needed once the Narcissist regains control of a situation.

Unless you understand what motivates an N to rage, you may find yourself feeling powerless and confused as you try to find logical reasons for your N's sudden bursts of anger. There is power in the realization of his/her anger as a desperate attempt to regain feelings of control.

Part Two

Chapter 10

The Power of Choice

I hope you are feeling the power of choice as you continue this journey of understanding and healing. Choice is something we take away from ourselves when we give our N's our own power. Without realizing it, we give up our rights and allow ourselves to be dictated by our N's. Remember, when we allow ourselves to be manipulated by others, we are handing over our power. We don't feel we have a choice in many matters concerning our N's. Instead of confronting the N, we often swallow our pride and don't even express our needs or ideas

Learning about NPD and N's helps us understand their actions and even predict what these acts will be. When they troll for OS or try to devalue us in order to regain a sense of false control, we realize what they are doing and why. Seeing through their façade helps us understand our choice to respond or ignore. To be given back the right to choose is very empowering! But you've only come midway. Stick around. It gets better!

A very young child views the world as an ideal place. There are super heroes that come and protect the good people from bad guys and a jolly fat man who travels the entire world in one night to give presents to well-behaved children. Parents tell their children that if they are good, wonderful magical things will happen. The N seems to be stuck in that childlike mentality. His emotional level may be compared to that of a toddler's. Being viewed as "good" is very important to the N. He views his true self in such contrast that he creates a better self...a good self. He believes that if he is good, wonderful things will happen to him. He wants others to see him as a "good" person, perhaps a father or a community leader. He believes in the existence of a perfect love and is determined to find it no matter what he has to experience in order to obtain it.

When the N meets a new woman, a woman who appears to possess admirable characteristics he desires, he is immediately drawn to her with the magical thinking that she could be "the one."

In the beginning of their relationship, the N sees strengths and qualities in his partner he wishes to possess, so he immediately tries to convince her that they are meant to be together. His acute fear of abandonment intensifies his desire so he often rushes into things others would avoid in the early stages of relationships. He may tell his partner he is in love with her within weeks of meeting her. His need to secure the relationship and avoid abandonment drives him to become possessive, even with his partner's things. He may refer to her house as "home," or say "our car" instead of "your car." By establishing ownership right away, he feels he is securing his catch and decreasing his chance of being deserted. Ironically, when things go awry in the relationship, the N doesn't have an issue with abandonment, as he usually bolts, without looking back.

His disorder dictates his motivation, but he actually has the ability to refrain from acting upon that motivation. Some N's, through therapy, learn to control their urges or respond in healthier ways to situations, as they understand what drives their desires. While the N's first impulse may be to insult or devalue someone's achievement, through counseling he can learn to stifle that impulse and even react in a more appropriate way. Many N's refuse to seek counseling because they believe nothing is wrong with them. Those who do undergo therapy are often driven by the desire to expose a partner's flaws or shift the blame from themselves.

If a therapist refuses to make an N feel special or holds him responsible for the negatives in his relationship, the N usually will discontinue therapy. He will say the therapist was not "helping" him or was "clueless." Sometimes, however, a Narcissist will be able to charm his therapist and win him/her over. That type of patient/therapist relationship serves as supply for the N and he will continue therapy as long as that supply is available.

Those victimized often come to believe that an N is simply an insensitive player who takes what he wants and then discards it when he no longer has use for it. Convincing an N of this is much more difficult. His reality is warped and he actually views himself as the victim. In his distorted way of thinking, he has to suffer through many imperfect relationships and deal with insecure, clingy women who often "stalk" him after their relationships end, all because he is trying to find true love. Life seems so unfair to the N. He doesn't realize that his fear of abandonment, coupled with his fear of commitment, creates pain and insecurity in his partners. He is clueless to the fact that his lies and inconsistencies are what bring about the lack of trust in his relationships. Many times, the N actually believes the narratives he spins for himself are true; therefore, his lies become his reality.

Because the N appears sincere, generous and giving in the beginning of his relationship, he convinces his charmed partner that he believes he has found the perfect mate. She believes that she is the answer to his prayers and gets caught up in the euphoria of ideal love. She relaxes and begins to cultivate a relationship with him.

The fear of abandonment which we spoke of earlier causes the N to secure his relationship by charming or convincing his partner that she is "the one." Once she buys into his ardent affirmations, she commits herself to the relationship and to him. The N's fear of commitment causes him to back away at this stage. The hunt, the chase, and the manipulation are "highs" for the N. The possibility that someone as special as his partner could want him is what drives him to gain her possession. Once he has her, however, he convinces himself that she must be flawed to want someone like him and begins to notice things about her that weren't as obvious in the beginning of their relationship. However, when something goes wrong, the relationship is no longer "ideal" to the N. Once it is flawed, the relationship loses its value to him.

Ironically, the very things that attracted him to his partner initially have become the things that repulse him once she commits to him. What he has seen as strong independence morphs into stubborn pride. What he has viewed as impressive organizational skills become anal retentiveness. He justifies his initial blindness to her flaws by convincing himself that he had been in a vulnerable state of mind when he met her or that he allowed his physical attraction to her cloud his judgment. He feels embarrassed that he could have mistaken his attraction to her for his ideal partner, but he rationalizes that his weakened emotional state could have caused him confusion.

As the relationship begins to deteriorate (in his mind), the N plans his escape. He feels no empathy for his partner and now sees her as the "bad guy." She doesn't "get" him (he doesn't see how his inconsistencies in behavior could leave *anyone* with a lack of understanding). She is too needy (he is unaware that *he* has actually caused her insecurities by continuously pulling away from her). She is more concerned with her needs than his (how dare anyone have a life outside of catering to an N?). By staying with a flawed, self-serving, insecure, distrusting person, the N would be compromising *his* "integrity." He would feel smothered, overwhelmed and victimized. He would feel as if he were giving up any chance of ever finding ideal love. Since he ultimately puts himself and his needs first, the N doesn't hesitate to save himself from what he sees as a tortuous existence, and flees.

If the partner of an N is unaware of her disorder, he will naturally try to save what he sees as a fairy tale romance, at first. After all, he played the part of the prince, rescuing his princess from a troubled existence. But now as he continues to review the relationship, he will remember special feelings turning to confusion as his partner began to seem disappointed in him. He will recall trying to alter his behavior to please her, and how his attempts were futile. As he is forced to cope with her departure, he will be flooded with memories of lies, inconsistencies, failed attempts to recapture what he thought he had with her in the beginning of their relationship and doubts and insecurities that were spawned by her behavior. When he realizes she has moved on so quickly from their relationship, he will label her a player and feel used and devastated.

The N and his partner both feel victimized due to their different concepts of reality. However, the N has the ability to erase anything that no longer serves as narcissistic supply for her and unfortunately, that includes people. Her partner may take a much longer time to recover.

Material possessions, souvenirs from partners, people who have served as "good supply," music that reminds him of positive moments in his life and trophies representing achievements or accomplishments are all kept by the N as sources of secondary narcissistic supply. His efforts to discard and forget all sources of negative supply are equally as ardent as his efforts to hang onto the positive reminders. His ability to discard people he seemed to cherish at one time is not difficult to understand once you realize that people are mere objects to the Narcissist.

In many cases the N is a victim, and NPD shouldn't be taken lightly. However, there are those cases where the N *realizes* he is making bad choices, yet continues to make them anyway. And along the way many vulnerable, unknowing victims are cruelly wounded.

By this time, we hope things should be making more sense to you if you have been victimized. Perhaps you have discovered some missing pieces to the puzzle you were so painstakingly trying to assemble. Have you seen glimpses of your hurtful partner throughout these pages? If so, are you beginning to gain some understanding about his cruel actions? Though realizing that his cruelty wasn't intentionally directed at you is of some explanation, we know it doesn't offer complete comfort. When in the throes of heartache, however, after understanding that the N is afflicted with a personality disorder, and is seemingly at its mercy, many people tend to feel pity for him. Remember, though, not to pity the N for very long. Beware that although his motivations are spurred by his disorder, he is an adult, regardless of his childlike, emotional state of being. As an adult, he knows right from wrong and has the ability to make moral choices. By giving in to his cravings and cruelly using others, he demonstrates a weakness in his personality (one of his many character flaws). He can and must be held accountable for his actions regardless of the fact that he feels no remorse for them.

So don't waste sympathy on your N. Sure, he feels driven by the desire to obtain ideal love and feels he is at the mercy of those desires. While his mother may have given him too much or too little love, chances are she taught him right from wrong. Even if she failed in that area as well, adults don't become adults without being exposed to that knowledge somewhere along the way and they must be held responsible for their own actions. And even though he lives in a world of denial, and will probably never accept responsibility you can release *yourself* from it.

When you reach this point of realization, congratulate yourself on having come so far. You are gaining control and understanding. You are not the same dependent person you were when you began this journey. The best is yet to come!

Chapter 11

The Reflection Is Not Real

I hope you are now feeling strong and aware as you allow the stress you have felt earlier to roll away. Victims of N's often allow themselves to carry the guilt and responsibility of their failed relationships on their own shoulders. Eventually, that stress begins to show on the victims' faces as worry lines appear across their foreheads, dark circles and puffy bags show under their eyes, extra weight clings to their midsections or they develop an overall look of premature aging. This is just another example of how someone *else* assumes responsibility for the N's actions.

Did you ever notice how your N appeared quite young for her age? Why shouldn't she? She isn't the one carrying the weight of her negative actions. She simply discards the negatives and doesn't look back. Each new day is a new beginning for her. She constantly reinvents herself. This is especially true for Somatic N's. They spend a lot of time grooming and caring for their bodies.

The N simply observes life, even her own experiences, as if she were watching a movie. Sometimes that "movie" is fun and exciting, so she sticks around to see how it will play out. Other times the "movie" is boring, so she walks out…just as one would leave a movie theater…with no commitment and no sense of loss.

Walking in and out of "movie theaters," watching and participating in particular scenes and constantly writing new scripts and acting out new roles…all contribute to the Narcissist's warped sense of time. That is how he is able to walk away from his partner, play another role with his New Supply for a while and then walk back into his ex-partner's life as if no time has passed at all. To an N, time isn't viewed as a period of existence from one point to another but rather seen as a circle. There is no beginning and no end…only an endless search. If permitted, an N will walk back into someone's life after months, or even years, of being absent and try to revise the relationship as if no time has passed. He will continue to gather narcissistic supply there until he has procured new supply elsewhere and needs once again to make his exit.

The "ageless" Dorian Gray in Oscar Wilde's novel, where the character is similar to the persona of an N, doesn't necessarily feel himself limited to partners within a specific age group. The world is his oyster. Many times, the N's partner feels the N is without morals or values because of his seeming lack of judgment concerning partners. However, supply is supply to the N, regardless of its packaging.

The N's love to be admired by *anyone*, regardless of age or gender… supply is what maintains their existence. An N doesn't view human beings as normal people do. Human beings are simply objects to the N…objects that exist to supply him with adoration, admiration, and proof of his superior existence.

Did you ever notice how your N seemed to thrive on *any* type of attention, regardless of age or gender? Did you ever find yourself questioning his sexuality? Chances are, if you confronted him with this possibility, he raged against you. N's are known to rage when they feel threatened with any type of exposure. He interprets any type of disagreement as criticism and becomes very defensive. When a normal person expresses anger it is often a reaction to some type of stress. For an N, rage isn't necessarily derived from anger-related stress. Often, the N is reacting to having felt slighted or criticized in some way. When he feels threatened, he will use rage as a defense mechanism to devalue the source of those threats.

Did you ever notice a time when you felt your partner overreacted to a situation and raged against you? At first, that type of reaction is unsettling and catches you off guard. You find yourself wondering, "Where did that come from?" Later, such outbursts become the "norm" and you learn to cower and become withdrawn in order to avoid that type of behavior. This is very typical behavior for partners of Narcissists. Your cowering behavior is not something you learned instantly. Many partners of N's have actually been associated with N's prior to meeting their partner, though they aren't always aware of this.

After becoming familiar with NPD, victims who then become sensitive to the personality begin to realize that there are many N's around them. Even their family members seem to be N's. The fact is that partners of N's were probably exposed to narcissism at an early age. An N may have even raised them.

Think about it for a few moments. Try to recall: did your father or mother have any of the narcissistic traits you have been reading about? Was nothing ever good enough for him/her? Did he/she rage at the slightest incident? If you brought home a "B" on your report card, did he/she tell you it could have been an "A?" Did you feel as if nothing you did measured up to his/her standards? Did you find yourself being obedient, passive and/or extraordinarily careful in order to "keep the peace?" If you answered, "yes" to some of these questions, it is quite possible that you were shaped at a very early age for your N and that having a relationship with him was not a chance occurrence.

Many negative conditions take place in a family where someone is afflicted with NPD. For example, in a family where the father has NPD, his kids fear him...he interprets that fear as respect. He claims that he prefers fear to love and strives to ensure that his children respect him above all else. To an N, any type of emotion is interpreted equally as supply. A narcissistic father would just as easily accept fear from his children, as he would love. Both emotions prove his existence and reinforce his delusions of omnipotence.

Can an N raise a mentally healthy child? You may be surprised that the answer to that question is a resounding "yes." But many times, N's breed N's, co-dependents, or even Inverted N's. An Inverted N (IN) is a co-dependent who relies exclusively on and actively seeks relationships with N's. They feel unfulfilled unless they are in a relationship with an N. Inverted N's aren't as common as co-dependents, because in order to qualify as an IN, one must feel empty and unsatisfied in relationships with any other personality types.

Most partners of N's tend to be co-dependents. They spend their relationships trying to "fix" things, trying to lift their partner's spirits and trying to morph into his version of the perfect woman. They buy into his belief of "ideal love" and fool themselves into believing they are part of a fairy tale romance. They find themselves spending countless hours and exorbitant amounts of energy working on ways to maintain that fairy tale existence.

Some partners of N's are N's themselves. Because N's have interactions rather than relationships, these tend to be the best partners for an N. Both use each other for supply. Neither partner expects love, nor puts "unrealistic" demands (such as commitment or loyalty) on the other. A relationship between two N's is more like a business arrangement. There is no love, but no love lost. This type of relationship can last as long as both partners are willing to use each other as secondary supply when necessary.

If you were narcissized by your partner, chances are *you* are not an N. Depending on how you are dealing with the situation, you may be "normal" or a co-dependent. A "normal" partner, upon realizing he or she has been narcissized, will walk away from the situation and count his or her blessings to be done with such a relationship. On the other hand, a co-dependent will invent ways to *cure* the N. Because of prior shaping to be the "fixer," the co-dependent will feel as if she holds some special key to unlock the madness. Such co-dependents will believe that if they can convince their partners of their personality disorders which developed during childhood due to circumstances of which the N may already be aware, the N will be willing to work toward recovery with the partner. Mistakenly, the partner believes the N will praise the partner for being the first person to bring that sort of awareness to them and they will once again be on top due to the partner's mighty power of "fixing things." The N's dream of "happily ever after" will finally be realized as she watches the partner's "true" self emerge and proves that the partner is lovable *as she or he is*…without having to create a "false" self.

Co-dependents are easy targets for people afflicted with NPD, because they share a similar type of magical thinking with the N. The N spends his life searching for an ideal love. With each new relationship he believes he has finally arrived, only to become disillusioned when the imperfections of the relationship are revealed. The co-dependent also believes in the possibility of ideal love, but rather than running away at the first sign of trouble as the N does, she stays and fights against all odds to maintain that love. Both the N and the co-dependent tend to create false realities in order to maintain their beliefs in the existence of a fairy tale romance. Ironically, the co-dependent believes if she can just open the N's eyes to his unrealistic beliefs, he can be healed and live out that fairy tale with her. However, a further irony is that if the N were capable of having empathy, and sincerely tried to point out his co-dependent partner's disillusionments, she would do whatever it took to correct those disillusionments. But alas, the N doesn't have empathy and is too into himself to be concerned about others, so the situation remains incurable.

The "love" between an N and a co-dependent is a tragic, doomed romance that is reminiscent of one of Shakespeare's sonnets. The first line of the sonnet reads, "When my love swears that she is made of truth, I do believe her, though I know she lies." Like the protagonist of the sonnet, the N "believes" his partner when she seems to reflect the false image he tries to project. The partner "believes" the N when he tells her she is the "love of his life" or that the call he just received was from a "friend." Throughout their relationship, the N and his partner continue to pretend things are better than they actually are. The last line of the sonnet states, "Therefore, I lie with her and she with me and in our faults by lies we flattered be." After understanding the interactions between an N and his co-dependent partner, the last line of the sonnet takes on a profound and sad meaning. Like the two lovers, the partner and the N live in their fantasy worlds and continue to flatter each other by encouraging their false selves until the relationship's imminent demise.

Do you recognize your partner in any of the information which we've been discussing? Do you see anyone else? We realize we have been giving you a lot of information to digest. But arming yourself with this information will enable you to understand your partner's motivations and spur your healing process. By accepting the possibility that your partner is afflicted with NPD, you allow yourself to look within and distinguish tendencies that may have attracted you to him. You will become aware once you recognize those tendencies and are able to train yourself against them. We hope you are feeling strong as you create the means for your stressors to roll away.

Chapter 12

Clarity...Understanding... Vision

We are sure you are now feeling more conscious of your relationship and all of its components, even the ones you hid from yourself. That is a good thing! As you continue studying NPD you will recognize how many people N's have affected and why this has affected you so strongly.

 Alanis Morissette's recording of a song entitled "Narcissus" expressed how her Narcissist "Boy" had been shaped by his mother to need attention and how he never claimed responsibility or really listened to his partner. She revealed that he never had to suffer any consequence, because he never stayed with anyone longer than ten minutes. Morissette mentions how talk of selflessness, healthiness or connectedness left him running for the door. Her lyrics also reflected her confusion as to why she still felt "affected by him." Many of her other songs give reference to the pain one suffers while being involved with an N. In her song entitled, "Head Over Feet," however, Alanis sings about someone who appears to have moved on and found a relationship with a healthy partner. She states,

"I am aware now." That *awareness* which she expresses, is the beginning of what eventually sets us free.

Once we realize that we are actually sacrificing ourselves in order to ensure the happiness of our partners, we can recognize that we are in an unhealthy relationship. We should not have to give up our own interests, friends or hobbies for anyone. Healthy relationships involve *both* partners making compromises when necessary; they require an exchange of give and take. Normal relationships are not one-sided. No one should feel as if he/she should be incredibly cautious about what the person says or does to avoid upsetting his/her partner. Partners should contribute equally in a relationship. There will be days when one partner feels it necessary to lift or encourage the other. Each and every day should not be about only one partner.

Moreover, if you find yourself jumping through hoops to please your partner on a daily basis, chances are something is not right. Awareness of these tendencies and being able to recognize narcissistic characteristics in your relationship can help you avoid becoming narcissized in the future.

If you are beginning a relationship, be aware that one of the telltale signs that your partner may be an N is a tendency to blame others for his mistakes or failures. When you first become involved with a person, it is a good idea to identify any narcissistic tendencies he may have. Check to see if he takes responsibility for his faults, or if he shifts the blame to someone else, such as his family members, his incompetent employees, the government, waiters, etc.

Another sign is his seemingly disrespect for your boundaries or when he treats you as an object for his own satisfaction. He might show up, unannounced, at your place and just assume you will accept his invitation to go on a date or spend the evening with him on such short notice. Be aware if he exhibits super-sensitivity and becomes slighted or insulted by situations that you consider exaggerated on his part.

His desire for control is another narcissistic sign. He may try to maintain control of every aspect of your relationship by ordering your food at a restaurant, interrogating you about your phone calls, or insisting upon being in charge of your finances. You may even feel as if you need to ask his permission to do things you would normally do on your own, such as visiting a friend or family member.

N's seem to be eager to become committed. They will say "I love you" early in their relationships and their partners will also hear professions such as, "You are the love of my life" or "This is my best relationship I've ever had."

You may notice that he is condescending or patronizing to you. He may be criticizing you while exaggerating your talents (devaluing and idealizing you).

He may have unrealistic expectations of the relationship and of you. He may tell you that you "make" him happy or "make" him feel good, only to later say that you "make" him angry or "make" him feel bad. We cannot "make" anyone feel anything.

 If you recognize some of the characteristics we've discussed, you are very likely in the company of an N and should immediately end the romance.

While in some cases it would be easy to disconnect from someone afflicted with NPD and avoid any future contact, it is not always possible. Perhaps the person is a family member with whom you must associate, even if only during special occasions or holidays. If you absolutely *have* to be associated with an N, you will need to learn some strategies that will assure your independence and serve as buffers against selfish assaults.

Since the N's entire world exists only in his mind, it is imperative that he remains in control at all times. This is why he surrounds himself only with individuals who are willing to reflect his false image. Therefore, people are only internal objects to him. They exist in his mind as characters he has written into his script and can be written out just as easily. By manipulating the characters in his mind, the N maintains control of his "universe." If his "puppets" were to break away from their strings and exist on their own, the Narcissist would feel as if he were losing control of his "world." Therefore, he would feel as if he were going insane in his world. That is why Narcissists carefully select their supply and avoid certain types of people altogether. People who are independent or "disobedient" challenge the Narcissist's belief that he is the center of the world and threaten to expose his real vulnerable self.

An N will rage at the slightest offense when he feels threatened. Because the partner of an N is usually caught off guard by his attacks, she doesn't always react in a defensive way. Her shock serves as narcissistic supply for him and he continues to rage against her whenever he feels threatened.

Some experts suggest that one way to deal with an N's rage is to *rage back*. He doesn't expect this and loses some of the control he feels he has over the situation. However, another method is to withhold emotion when reacting to his rage. This can be more effective, because the N interprets no attention as "no supply."

A good method to maintain control of situations involving your N is to remain neutral while in his presence. Conversations should be limited to necessary subjects and should be kept short and informative. Try not to show emotion whenever you feel angry or disgusted by his actions, which will be often. If he feels he is no longer able to evoke emotions or extract reactions, he will experience a loss of control.

When the N in your life is your partner or ex-partner, it is easier to follow these suggestions. If the N in your life is your parent, it is much more difficult.

Chapter 13

Handling Narcissistic Parents

Many children of N's experience feelings of never being "good enough," always falling short and having overall pangs of inadequacy. Narcissistic parents assume the role of "Most Important Person" and expect their children to help them maintain that status. If a child shows affection or admiration for other family members, a narcissistic parent will devalue the other family members and remind the child where his loyalties should lie. A narcissistic parent often feels in competition with his own children. She or he will devalue his/her children, especially if they appear to possess self-confidence. An N lacks self-confidence and views it as a threat in others. While the N may be drawn to partners who seemingly possess self-confidence, he/she will eventually envy and mimic that characteristic. The N will eventually devalue the partner, ridding the person of self-confidence as he forces him or her to mirror the N's true self.

The N's need to remain in control drives him to "humble his children"; this ensures the safety of his powerful position. When the children of an N are very young, they pose no threat of individuality. They are mere furniture to the N. He uses them as supply to gain praise for his incredible child-rearing skills. He will show them off only as a way to reflect his false self. He will let the public know what a great caregiver he is and how much he adores his children. Once the child of an N becomes "an individual," (begins to think for himself) he may no longer be considered an extension of the N or necessary as supply and may be ignored or neglected. In some cases, an N will tell his child he is no longer his/her parent or that he is disconnecting from his child's life and will no longer be "involved." This can be a devastating blow to a child...causing narcissistic injury. The child may even begin creating his own "false" self, realizing he has no one to depend on but himself at that point. This is understandable as the father figure is seen as the head of the family...providing for it, teaching values, and showing unconditional love. When a father chooses to remove himself from his child in such a way, he withdraws that "light" from his child's world, leaving behind the darkness of insecurity and vulnerability. When a child believes that his own father can disconnect from his life, he realizes he is totally on his own. His fear of abandonment causes him to create his own security, relying on the only person he knows for sure won't disappoint him...himself. Other times, the child will become clingy and insecure, and constantly try to "measure up" and "regain" his/her father's approval.

Sometimes, the N will use physical or verbal abuse as a form of supply and continue to extract this from his child even after the child learns to think independently from his parent. Psychologists have explained incestuous relationships with N's as "the closest thing to making love to oneself." Sexual abuse is also used as supply for certain Narcissists.

Children of N's often spend their lives feeling inadequate. Some research indicates that children of N's are subconsciously drawn to narcissistic partners in an effort to correct what went wrong in their childhoods.

Because they learned at an early age how to cower, withdraw and avoid narcissistic rage, co-dependents appear more tolerant of their partner than a "normal" person would. Subconsciously, they are already used to devaluation, so it becomes easy for them to buy into the negativity their partners insist they possess. While the N tries to obtain the "ideal love" she was denied during her childhood, her partner tries to win "undeserving" approval. Together they participate in this dance macabre until its fatal termination.

If your N is a parent, be aware that it is difficult to disconnect and even more difficult to adhere to the "No Contact" rule. Here is an example of a letter written by the child of a narcissistic parent in order to gain closure from their relationship and achieve healing.

Dear Dad/Mom,

I spent my life trying to convince you that I was worthy of your approval, but always seemed to come up short. Before I learned about Narcissistic Personality (NPD), I thought something had to be wrong with me since my own parent thought I had so many faults. When you would accuse me of lying, it would always break my heart because I worked so hard to be a good and honest person. When you told me I talked just to hear the sound of my own voice or twisted my words in order to win arguments, I did not understand you were merely transferring your own attributes onto me. I have since learned that people afflicted with NPD believe that everyone thinks the same way they do so they are constantly transferring their own negative traits onto others. Narcissists see their interactions with people as self-serving and assume everyone's associations with people are just as selfish.

You "playfully" put me down, even in front of my friends and you became upset if I reacted negatively to it. You told me I was "overly-sensitive." Hmmm, "overly-sensitive,"...you guessed it, another characteristic of people afflicted with NPD. This is yet another example of transference of negative traits.

If I ever credited anyone for positive contributions in my life, you would devalue that person, reminding me of all the wonderful things you had done for me.

When I brought home a school project that had been praised by a teacher, you would tell me that you had created similar projects when you were in school, and of course, they were much better. Whenever I was elected to do something in school or when I received awards for something, you would "jokingly" say things like, "Were they that hard up to find a winner?" This would have been okay if you had then complimented me or praised me for my accomplishment. I never understood why you never praised me or why you felt the need to insult me until I began researching NPD. Now so many things make sense to me.

I learned that if the child of a Narcissist were ever involved with a "special" event, the Narcissist would either ignore it or try to devalue it in some way. This would allow the N to squelch the special status of the situation. Special qualities are limited to the Narcissist. His jealousy, even of his own children, will prevent him from acknowledging special qualities in others.

Whenever I was sick I was expected to "suck it up" or "tough it out" and was never allowed to complain. However, when you got sick the whole world had to stop and cater to you. This was always very confusing to me as I never understood why the same rules didn't apply to you.

As I studied NPD, I learned that Narcissists believe that they are "special"; apparently, nobody else is allowed that special status, not even their own children. The same rules that apply to emotionally healthy individuals never apply to a Narcissist. He expects everyone to stop and take notice of him when he gets sick, even though he sees that as a weakness in others.

During holidays I never understood why you seemed so gloomy and depressed. I had convinced myself that during your childhood something terrible must have happened around the holidays that caused you to dread them each year. Then I learned that many Narcissists resent the holidays because those particular days are not about them! A Narcissist needs to feel in control of every situation and needs to believe that he has a direct impact on everyone's mood. During the holiday season, people express joy and excitement that is not directly related to the Narcissist, robbing him of his false sense of control. He will often pout or react very negatively, bringing down everyone's mood. Once he has successfully changed the atmosphere, he feels back in control and may even go about trying to "lift" everyone's spirits. After all, if he causes their moods to shift, then it becomes about him, again. This explains why we had so many crazy Christmases!

All I ever wanted was your approval or praise. Nothing I seemed to do was ever good enough. I wanted a loving parent and you shaped me into your servant, and I became the servant of any Narcissist I happened to come in contact with later in my life. This resulted in my servicing others by giving them their much-needed narcissistic supply.

When I didn't gain approval from you, I would set out on a mission to gain approval from another Narcissist…any Narcissist. Because of my shaping, I needed to be validated as a good person by someone with traits similar to yours. Regardless of my accomplishments and success, I still needed someone else to tell me I was a good person.

I am now learning to look within and guess what? Rather than hiding from myself and getting wrapped up in the lives of others, I am actually getting to know who I really am. I am spending time with myself and I am finding that I am in good company!

Because I have realized that you are at the mercy of your disorder, I no longer need you (or anyone else) to validate me; I realize you cannot.

Now that I am getting to know myself and what makes me tick, I realize that I am the only one with that kind of "inside information," therefore, only I can validate myself. So far, so good.

In order for me to move on I want to tell you that you're forgiven.

Catherine

Part Three

Part Three

Chapter 14

Taking Back Control

Your journey so far has led you to some eye opening discoveries. I hope you have learned as you progressed along the way that you don't need someone else's approval in order to feel validated.

People with co-dependent tendencies look to others for self-validation. They feel they need someone to tell them that they are, "smart enough," "attractive enough," "successful enough" and "worthy enough."

Ironically, if the people from whom they wish to receive that validation are N's, they usually do not possess those qualities, themselves.

Think about the person with whom you're involved who may be completely self-obsessed. Now, armed with your knowledge of NPD, take a closer look at him/her.

- The "false" self of the N is created with lies (therefore, why would you need *him* to validate the fact that *you* are an honest person).
- An N views human beings as nothing more than disposable objects from which she obtains the supply necessary to maintain

her lie…her "false self." Who would want validation from someone who doesn't even value human life?

- After discarding their partners, N's will return for supply as many times as they are allowed. They say whatever they need to convince their partners that they intend to "make it work this time," only to discard them sooner the following time. How can you expect an N to know want *you* want when he doesn't even know what *he* wants?

- He/she is lacking so much in self-confidence that he/she is forced to reinvent himself/herself on a daily basis. The N mimics the confidence he/she sees in others.

- The "Jekyll and Hyde" aspects of a Narcissist's personality are horrendous; especially when he demonstrates extreme changes in moods within a very short period of time. Ask yourself if you really want identity-validation from a person who has no true identity of his own?

- Because N's will extract from *any* supply available, their standards or tastes in beauty are subject to change as often as the supply is. He or she must convince himself/herself that *he/she* is the definition of true beauty. Ask yourself if you really value your N's opinion about *your* looks knowing what "beauty" lies within the N?

Most N's seem to have very few "true" friends. First of all, it is difficult for an N to maintain long-term friendships, because he is constantly reinventing himself. His dishonest and unpredictable behavior drives most people away. The N keeps supply and secondary supply on hand. There may even be a few people who cling to him or her, because they are desperate for validation. But even family members tend to avoid the N when possible. Other "long-term friends" tend to be people who do not live within close proximity of the N (possibly not even in the same state). This makes it easier for the N to keep his/her "false" self alive, thus maintaining long-term interactions with those people.

Old age is often very lonely for the N. He spends so much time trying to satisfy himself during his younger years that as he gets older, he pushes others away. He may be too "tired" to go to his children's ballgames or too "busy" to spend quality time with friends and family members when he is in the prime of his life, because most of his time will be spent acquiring and maintaining narcissistic supply.

As she ages, the Narcissist loses many of the tools she used for obtaining supply. If she is a Somatic N, when her looks fade with age, her body will no longer gain compliments she seeks; she will lose her sex drive and her potential for supply will diminish greatly. Due to her negative behavior, most of her "friends" and family members will have removed themselves from her presence years before she grows old. Her propensity toward negativity will ensure her bitter existence as she watches the final scenes of her life play out in "undeserved" mistreatment and doom.

If the N ever has a visitor in her twilight years, instead of enjoying the company, she will spend time complaining to her visitor about how no one ever comes to see her. She may recount her misfortunes and mistreatment by others. Once again, her exaggerated sense of entitlement will lead her to believe that *she* is the victim. She will curse her children for not being loyal and loving and for ignoring her during her old age. Her memories of their childhood will be about how much she did for them and how ungrateful they were in return. She will mention how she hopes to stay alive long enough to see justice served and to see what will be reaped from what had been sown.

The "false" self of an N can be compared to the surface of a flooding lake. The golden sun reflects its sparkling beauty just as the beautiful image of the N is reflected by his current supply. Delving deeper into the lake, one sees a darker side that's filled with things that aren't as pretty. The "pretty" side of the N is composed of lies that he must forever cultivate in order to maintain. Meanwhile, he pushes his "ugly" side deeper into hiding.

We mentioned earlier that there are ways to heal yourself from your "N-Fliction." Once the one-dimensional character of the N's "false" self is revealed, he no longer poses a threat or holds a position of importance or power.

Regardless of whether you are co-dependent or not, your first step is to look within yourself to identify possible characteristics which may have attracted you to relationships with N's. Becoming aware of the "inner workings" of the N and becoming "mindful" of yourself, help you gain back the control you gave to others by allowing them to validate your character. You begin to "see the forest!"

Carl Jung, the famed psychologist, theorized that co-dependency is brought about by society. At birth, the baby is labeled in pink or blue as male or female and begins fulfilling society's gender-expectations. Jung believed that we were intended to be complete within ourselves and that we all possess a male and female persona; but, depending on our gender, we are forced to bury our "other half" as society shapes us into our culture's definition of that gender. He believed that this is why we sometimes feel "something is missing" or that we need to find our "other half" in order to be complete.

Regardless as to whether Jung's theory of our dual personas has complete validity, his belief that society is partially responsible for our co-dependent tendencies is right on the mark, especially where women are concerned. Historically, in western and some other societies, women have been forced into domestic roles and excluded from many opportunities. Society defined marriage and child rearing as the primary purpose of a woman's existence, and it was typically necessary for her survival. The struggles facing a woman who did not marry—for whatever reasons—were challenging. Therefore, much of a woman's time on this earth was spent preparing herself to marry a man, successfully fulfilling the responsibilities of marriage and then teaching her daughters how to do the same.

You may say, "Yes, but those antiquated beliefs about women are a thing of the past and not relevant to modern women, who enjoy most of the opportunities available to men, are free to marry, remain single, have a long-term partner, or whatever they choose. Today, at least idealistically, a woman can freely choose whether or not to have children and a single woman can even choose to raise children on her own through artificial insemination or adoption."

While all of that is true, society still tends to stereotype women, and the pressure to fulfill stereotyped roles continues to be powerful. The more clearly women see the external beliefs and assumptions society makes regarding them, the more powerfully they can define and refine their own beliefs regarding themselves as individuals. Whether they choose to be a full-time homemaker, pursue a full-time career or be a working mother, women need to be able to discover the paths that are right for them rather than be forced into molds created by societal pressures.

Have you ever noticed how billions of dollars are spent each year in advertising to teach women how to catch and hang onto a man? Society has not only accepted, but also helped to create the idea that a woman's role is as a submissive caregiver whose positive attributes are valued as mere offerings for a man. Nowhere is this more evident than in the media, where women are stereotyped and beauty is defined in the strictest of terms. Some magazines appeal to women readers by promising to inform them of ways to "lose five pounds to catch his eye," "find his pleasure zones," or "keep him satisfied." The pressure on women to be beautiful in this culture is oppressive, but it can be especially damaging when the underlying message becomes "you must be beautiful—as *we* define it—to be accepted by men." As a result, societal values regarding beauty and self-acceptance can influence women to believe that they must be different from their true selves to be accepted by others. This can begin to lay the groundwork for the formation of co-dependency. Furthermore, these values can influence women to believe that men must accept them—or give their approval—because of the superior position of men in the world.

During World War II, women were needed in the work force to maintain jobs left by men who had gone to war. We finally got a glimpse of the multidimensional value of women as they successfully maintained those jobs. Upon their return from war, however, many men expected their wives to go back to their traditional roles and perform earlier tasks as if nothing had changed. The traditional role of woman as "helpmate" was strongly entrenched. Though much has changed in the last fifty years, the far-reaching impact of this traditional role still impacts the lives of many women, and complete equality has yet to be attained.

The majority of high-paying jobs are still held by men, and even in clubs where women are accepted as members, there are unspoken rules as to their positions. Thus there are many unrealistic expectations placed upon women in society...it often seems that the men are still the ones "running the show." Perhaps this is most visible in the dual roles many working women are expected to fulfill: that of breadwinner and domestic servant. Many working women have been expected to retain their position as subservient caregiver while holding down a full-time job no less demanding than their husband's. Though this arrangement is unfair, many women do not question their "duty" to serve their husband

and/or family in this way, and many men do not question the division of labor because that's the way it was with their parents.

The next time you watch a television program, notice how few television commercials market household products to men. Cleaning the house, preparing meals and shopping for groceries are stereotypically portrayed in the media as the domain of the woman. What's more, even if they are employed outside the house, women are frequently shown as the primary "errand runner" for the family, adding the role of "soccer mom" in a minivan to "career woman." These societal roles can make women vulnerable to co-dependent relationships, for they foster a relational inequality. This is not to say that every working mother who does most of the housework and drives the kids to soccer practice is co-dependent. However, many women do feel trapped and overwhelmed in their assumed domestic roles, yet are afraid to assert themselves and discuss a more fair division of labor. When a person accepts relational inequality without attempting to negotiate toward a balance of power and individuality, co-dependency is at risk. The N is instinctively drawn to the type of individual who will accept this kind of relationship, since he cannot survive in a relationship with a partner who demands equality.

Isn't it interesting that even our society's materialistic values often reflect the traditional roles imposed on women? A man has an unlimited supply of "toys" available for *his pleasure,* just as designer clothing and luxurious accessories are offered to a woman as ways to make her more attractive to him or more desired by him - in other words, also for *his pleasure*. While it's true that more and more women are breaking stereotypes and defining their own lives, many women feel "stuck in a rut" and can't even visualize what they want for themselves…much less understand how to make it happen.

In many ways society has historically defined women in ways that have shaped them into developing a co-dependency, into accepting inequality and sacrificing individuality in order to obtain and maintain a relationship with a man. While parents are usually blamed for the creation of co-dependent personalities, many societies contribute to the disorder, assuring its continued existence. Just as the parent of a co-dependent may continue to raise the bar, making him or her feel inadequate, society continues to expect women to morph into super-model, mop-wielding, sex addicts with a fine grasp of the culinary arts. And what about those women who feel they *have met* the criteria society has set for them? Do they feel as if they have arrived…made it? Once they have starved themselves into a size six dress, memorized the Kama Sutra, and discovered fifteen ways to prepare potatoes, do they feel they can finally meet their Maker in peace?

Remember, some of the most important questions you must ask yourself after being in a relationship with an N is: why you allowed him or her to treat you so badly; why you so often allowed his or her needs to take priority over your own; why you absorbed so much disrespect? How could you so willingly give away your power and individuality to pursue a relationship with this person? These questions can only be answered when you understand how past pressures from family and society affected your choices. It can be difficult to form healthy, functional relationships because society's preconceived notions of what a woman or man should be and how she or he should live get in the way of personal clarity and self-awareness.

Throughout a woman or man's life, she or he is confronted many times with the challenge to discover and honor their true self, or to conform to the pressures from family and society. This begins at a young age in the family, where messages about what it means to be a man or woman are first received. Whether spoken or unspoken, these messages are internalized and impact young girls' and boys' sense of self. In some cases the pressure to conform to these stereotypes is so extreme that the child has little choice but to live according to these stereotyped roles in order to survive. As a child, Karen, whom we'll discuss next, lived by such rules.

Karen learned at an early age that she had a long list of chores to complete each day. Her mom said that everyone in her family of five had to "pull his or her share of the load." Karen knew this to be true, but she also knew that her mother lived in fear just as she, her brothers and sisters did, for if the house wasn't clean or dinner wasn't ready when her dad got home, he got very angry. When daddy got angry, everybody paid the price. Karen knew he worked hard all day, and she saw how tired he was when he got home, and as the oldest she realized that she had a special responsibility to help.

Karen learned what time to expect daddy home, and got very good at anticipating his wishes and needs so he wouldn't get angry. Karen's mom pointed out that Karen was good at cheering up her daddy and she had to admit that her mother was right. It always seemed to work out best for her when Karen did what her daddy wanted, especially if she did it before he even asked her.

Karen never caused any problems at home. She was such a nice, easygoing girl. One time she wanted to try out for the school play with some of her friends, but her daddy yelled at her and said no one could drive her to rehearsal. She realized later never to ask for anything right before dinner, or after dad had downed four beers. She learned other survival skills that kept her from getting in trouble, and tried to pass them on to her younger siblings but they wouldn't always listen to her...this caused them to get the worst of it when daddy got angry. Daddy called Karen his "special sweetie," because she was so good at cooking his favorite meals and bringing him his beer. He always said she'd make somebody a good wife some day, and eventually Karen began to understand that her father's notions of a woman's role in life made him unconcerned that she was barely passing in school . . .

Karen essentially had to become numb to her own feelings and needs to survive in her childhood home. She developed a sense of identity based on helping others (specifically, a man) and her "true self" became so distant and faded it would take a lifetime of digging to re-discover what had been buried. Karen's mother was also trying to survive a difficult situation in which she felt trapped, and probably shared childhood experiences that led her to believe that she was being a good mother to Karen… that she was teaching her daughter how to get by in the world.

The reality was that if Karen continued on this path and did not somehow learn how to choose her own path, it would be very difficult for her to form relationships in which she did not act out the script written for her during her childhood. She would always be the *helper*, giving up her rights and fearing the loss of her loved ones' approval. The positive feelings she felt upon receiving approval from others came like imposters and took the place of her true feelings about herself and her place in the world. Since she did not realize she needed to discover her true self, she never knew that was what she really craved. Instead she always sought to feel needed by getting approval from others.

Ironically, had Karen not complied to her role as helper, had she become a rebellious teen and moved out of her parents' house to pursue her own path, she may have led a healthier life. When a person of either gender begins to ignore his or her true feelings to be accepted by others, the fear of rejection can grow, which in turn fuels the desire to feel accepted. This intense desire to feel accepted often becomes an overwhelming "need" as that becomes ever more disconnected from the true self. Here is a case study which could provide a glimpse into Karen's future.

Harry, who has a similar history, tells his story:

"It used to bother me when Angie got angry and snapped at me for no reason, but I always tried to avoid an argument so I never said anything, or would try to cheer her up. I thought it might change after we were married, but it didn't so I guess I just got used to it. My friends tell me that I shouldn't let her talk

to me like that, but I usually don't even notice it. I sometimes remember how I used to feel about it, however, when I hear my twelve-year old son talk to me the same way..."

Assertiveness is very difficult for a person with co-dependent tendencies. Conflict is very threatening and it could mean the loss of feeling accepted. To avoid risking rejection, the co-dependent is willing to give up his/her rights, allow boundaries to be crossed, or even suffer abuse at the hands of another—all for the sake of maintaining the "relationship." This works out very nicely for the N, who cannot tolerate being confronted by another, and who demands maintaining a position of superiority in the relationship. Meanwhile, the co-dependent becomes ever more alienated from his/her true self, increasing the desperate need to accommodate others to feel accepted.

In *Reviving Ophelia*, author Mary Pipher describes how many young girls are "traumatized" during their development between elementary and high school years because of damaging societal pressures. It is perhaps at this point that girls are most strongly confronted with the stereotypes of womanhood. Too often, it seems the freedom to be a spontaneous, fun-loving child who knows nothing other than to be herself is replaced with confusion, sadness and anger as the child is bombarded with society's expectations of what a young woman should be.

Others may suddenly consider behavior and values that were previously considered "okay" to be unacceptable. Childhood friends may suddenly change social groups as they try to assimilate these new external pressures. Adults may reinforce stereotypes as they try to prepare young girls for the "real world demands of womanhood." Little girls learn at very young ages what "a boy likes." Some mothers unwittingly train their daughters to please males with statements like, "Don't disagree with people like that...boys won't like you" or "Don't wear that shirt...boys don't find that type of clothing attractive." In *Reviving Ophelia*, Pipher suggests that:

Girls become "female impersonators" who fit their whole selves into small, crowded spaces. Vibrant, confident girls become shy, doubting young women. Girls stop thinking, "Who am I? What do I want" and start thinking, "What must I do to please others?"

Too often, women and men have accepted unrealistic expectations that are heaped upon them by society and reinforced by their parents or caregivers as the "norm"…and that's *not* okay!

Believing you are incomplete without a partner reveals inadequacies commonly felt by people who are co-dependent. Societal pressures and childhood emotional injuries can be recognized as contributing factors to your co-dependent tendencies. When you become self-aware and feel complete *on your own*, you can choose to be in a relationship for healthier reasons…or choose to be content alone.

Your next step toward healing is learning to gain validation *from yourself*. If you were conditioned to doubt your positive qualities due to constant devaluation from an important person in your life, you will instinctively question those qualities, regardless of what you *know* to be true. Your N was attracted to your positive traits initially, but used your weaknesses and your co-dependent tendencies, to keep you doubting them. This allowed him to maintain control over you. You take back that control when you realize that you *still* possess those wonderful qualities.

When you reach this point of self realization, heed this advice:

Let your accomplishments whisper your validation. Sometimes we get so caught up in what we are *not*, that we forget what we *are*. Once you realize that you don't need to be validated by someone else, you begin to break the chains that bind you to your abusers.

Look within; that little child who always looked to *others* for validation has moved beyond that place of dependence in so many ways. It is time to move into the light of independence, self-confidence and out of the shadows of fear and self-doubt. You don't need someone to tell you that you are okay. You already *know* that. Accept it. Become aware of who you really are. Though this fundamental life change can be very frightening, it is actually safer to live life authentically and confidently than it is to give away the power of your self-worth by allowing others to define it for you. You now know from life's painful experiences that from this day forward you *must* look within for your identity, your validation, and your self-worth. This will perhaps be the most important choice of your life, and you must make this choice many times each day. Remember, it took you years to learn to let others define you—it will take all of your determination to learn to define yourself, and discover a new way of living.

Think about your positive attributes and make a list of them. Claim those positives about yourself and spend some time alone...getting to know *you*. Before long, you will realize you are in good company and will no longer feel the need to hide from yourself in others.

After you become aware of characteristics that draw you to narcissistic people and recognize your caregivers and society as possible contributors to your co-dependency, you begin to take back control by learning to self-validate and are ready for step three...*letting go of the fairy tale*. You will recognize why you feel attached to the "happily ever after" theme and the prince or princess character. Connect childhood influences to reasons you feel a need to romanticize your relationships. Accept the possibility that you may have experienced Stockholm syndrome and stayed in abusive relationships because of their familiarity. Your partner devalued you many times...disrespected you and then discarded you. STILL, you felt it necessary to excuse his/her behavior and "believed" he/she would change.

Chapter 15

Gaining Perspective

As you progress in your study of Narcissistic Personality Disorder, you may notice some words used in an almost clinical, non-personal way describing the Narcissist's characteristics and behavior patterns. This can be very frustrating as you try to relate your situation to your partner's actions to gain further understanding. Here is a less clinical explanation, one to which you can relate as you continue to unfold the dark mysteries concerning your partner's behavior.

Have you felt as if your partner acted cruelly or insensitively by fondly recounting stories of his or her previous partners? What you may not have understood is that a Narcissist lives inside his or her mind…*always.* Their past partners are just parts of the script they are writing. There is no real concept of time to the N, so the stories they tell about partners from years in the past are still the same to them…fresh supply.

His warped idea of time is an important concept to understand. You have more than likely experienced it, yourself, when you recounted fond memories of your ex-partner, only to wonder, *Did that actually happen a year ago? Seems like just last week!* Imagine living *only* in your imagination. That is why the Narcissist is able to talk about past relationships as if they occurred just yesterday. "Real time" doesn't exist for him.

Try to accept the fact that an N doesn't live in "real life," but in her mind. She may experience the same situation as someone but "play" it differently in her mind and that is how she will remember it. Have you ever had her tell you *her* version of something that happened, yet it was completely different from the way you had experienced it? That is how she "played" it when it occurred…so for her, that *is* the "real" version of what happened.

We know it is hard to take his mistreatment of you in an impersonal way, but you must let go of some of the anger and confusion and realize that *you* are not really even there when you are with your partner. When you are having sex with him, you could be *anyone*, in any number of scenarios going on in his mind at that time. The same is also true in other situations. When you are with him, you are being manipulated whether you notice it, or not. You are saying what he wants and doing what he wants as part of *his play*. Once you stop being a two-dimensional character and begin to voice your own opinions, which "go against the script," you threaten his carefully constructed "reality" and are no longer useful as supply. He will then replace you with "another version" to play your part in that scene. This "new version" will quickly dismiss you as someone who "couldn't make him happy because…" as she begins to play the role of "ideal woman" in his play. When he tells you to leave him alone because he has finally "found happiness," he isn't telling *you* that…he is telling it to *your character*.

Now you are learning how things work for him. From the beginning, when the N splits and forms a "better self," he begins to live in his fantasy world. In his fantasy world he controls the characters, assuring that he will never again have to feel the pain he suffered which caused him to "split" in the first place. In his safe "new world" there are very few main characters; his "false" self is the star, there is the "bad character" that caused him his initial emotional injury, and finally, his "ideal partner" who rescues him from the "bad character" and helps him live in his perfect, pain-free world.

The N gets to play his "false" self. That is too difficult a role for *anyone else* to play. And you actually get to play the roles of *both* the "bad character" *and* the "ideal woman" before your part in the production is eventually terminated. In the beginning, you step into the play as the "ideal partner"…the "perfect fit"…the "woman of his dreams" that "rescues" him from the pain he has suffered from the "bad character."

Once you realize that *you* never really existed to him, you can better understand his actions. You were merely "solicited" to play the role of an ongoing character for him. You were "chosen" because of traits and characteristics you possess which "fit the role." That is why he seemed to *know* you very early in your relationship. He *knew* your role / character because he created it.

While most partners of the N will share many characteristics, some will bring something unique or different to the table…or the *stage*. When this happens, those characteristics are simply incorporated into his or her idea of a "perfect partner." This explains why your N may not remember *specifics* about each partner, but can recall general qualities and why he may mix up those unique traits, recalling your endearing dimples…the ones you don't have.

We equate being discarded with being "thrown away." This can be a devastating blow, regardless of our insecurities or co-dependent tendencies. But we must remember that *we* are not being discarded. The "bad character"…the one that *initially* emotionally scarred the Narcissist, is the one being "thrown away." The N has to relive that act

of "good conquering evil" as many times as he or she has to keep the
"ideal partner" fresh in his/her mind.

The truth is, you were not the one discarded nor were you the one
being "adored." You stepped in to play the role of "ideal partner" and
were eventually demoted to the role of "bad character," then "let go" as
a new actress was chosen to replace you. If she becomes a "method
actor" and takes her role too seriously, the N feels he cannot be responsible for that. Many women before you and after you will step up to play
the role of "ideal partner," each one hoping she will "play it better" than
the one before her. None of them realize that the character already
exists in its perfect form, in the N's mind; they don't realize that they are
merely objects helping to keep her "animated."

Imagine someone holding Barbie and Ken dolls, making them
interact while saying and doing whatever they want. That is the way it is
for an N as he interacts with people. When "Barbie" gets damaged it gets
replaced, but because the N is the only one he "trusts" not to rebel or
expose his "true" self, he is *always* Ken, so he has to continuously reinvent his "false" self. Therefore, he is forced to maintain his character
"mentally." Even the N, outside of his "false" world and his mind, is only
an object. He uses his body just as he uses other "objects" as supply, to
continue the world he created in his head.

I hope this helps you understand why your partner may have
seemed so insensitive at times. He or she created an "ideal partner." That
partner lives in the N's mind as the perfect one. Why would anyone *create* negative characteristics for the "perfect" partner? Would the "perfect
partner" accuse you of lying? Would the perfect partner question your
authority? Would the perfect partner have PMS or mood swings?
Absolutely not! Therefore, when the "object" or actor playing the role of
"perfect partner" tries to incorporate any of those negative characteristics, the Narcissist, the creator, rebels and eventually discards the non-

compliant object. The puppet is not allowed to break away from its strings or to write its own lines. That doesn't fit into the N's created world. Therefore, someone who will comply replaces the old partner.

That is another reason co-dependents are such good supply for an N. They are taught at an early age not to "rock the boat," to disregard their own feelings, and to keep quiet about what bothers them. This allows Ns to continue writing scenes for them as ideal partners. They are not allowed to exist outside the N's mind.

The N's insensitive reputation is magnified when he discards his partners without showing interest or concern for their feelings. But to the Narcissist, he isn't discarding his *ideal partner*. As always, she is still there in his mind. He is simply discarding the replaceable object that helped animate her.

It becomes easier to understand the N's seemingly selfish or cruel actions once you realize that the N views himself as an object with which to gain supply, and those around him as supply that enable the production of his "play."

Though the N is only one character in his play, his character can be the "good father" in some scenes or the "responsible citizen" in others. He manipulates his "supply" in order to achieve the role he desires. For example, when he wants to play "the martyr," he will "set the scene" and manipulate the situation…perhaps by not being home on his birthday or missing certain calls of congratulation. This allows him to "be the bigger person" and "forgive" those who have "slighted" him. The players in his scene will feel guilty that they weren't able to recognize the Narcissist on his "big day," so without realizing it, they "play the scene" *as the Narcissist intended*. The N wants his partner to attempt to make it up to him by fawning over him and making him feel "special." Those manipulated slights are entirely different from the slights brought on by someone "outside of character" threatening to "expose" the N.

Because of his warped concept of time and of human beings, the N often uses different people simultaneously to play the role of "perfect partner" in his script. Some people would consider this being unfaithful to one's partner, but the N doesn't see it that way because each of his women has a hand in maintaining the existence of his "perfect partner;" his partners are just "doing their job" and he *is* remaining faithful to the "ideal" woman in his mind.

Of course his "true" self is aware of the difference between right and wrong. When his partner forces him to see "glimpses of reality" by going against her script and pointing out his inconsistencies and faults by accusing him of infidelity, he is faced with the terrifying possibility of losing his "false" self and his "control."

His "glimpse of reality" includes a horrifying glimpse of his "true" self, he begins another series in efforts to "justify his behaviors," explain his actions, project his negative actions onto others, or blame them for causing him to do such vile things that go against his "character"…his "false" self.

The explanations of the N's behavior aren't for his partner but for himself. The partner, after all, is just an interchangeable object to him. The N's explanations are for *him* to reinforce his "false" self and to "walk off the pain" caused by a disobedient object.

The N "borrows" people to serve as objects that represent the characters in his mind. He has always (since his splitting) lived this way…it is what he *knows*. So, he feels *entitled* instead of feeling as if he is using or deceiving someone. He doesn't see the "discarding" in the same way his victims do because he isn't really discarding his ideal partner (the perfect woman/character that rescued him from the bad character). Different objects/people represent *her*, but she is always a part of the picture, never discarded. In the N's mind, the "bad character" really only gets discarded *once* and he lives happily, with his ideal partner.

Human beings are not supposed to be able to understand the concept of "infinity" when referring to time. However, the N's warped image of time allows us a glimpse into that idea. The N will tell his partner a story about how someone had flirted shamelessly with him and he'll repeat the *same story* years later to another partner as if it had recently happened. Because of the N's distorted sense of time, the story had actually occurred recently in his mind.

The N is a role-player. Because of the disorder he plays the main part in his created universe. This is a God-like role. The Creator of the universe is said to have created the world and brought it into existence. The N feels he is "omnipotent" and "omniscient" and very unique and special. He believes his word to be "the gospel." In his own mind he describes his "false" self as real, because he *says* it is. He even "creates" people in his "false" image to live in his world. His creations are supposed to live by *his* rules... follow his "commandments"...and if they refuse, they are "cast out" to live in a place that *doesn't include the N*, which in the N's psyche, would surely be Hell.

This type of "role-playing" is extreme and dangerous, because it becomes the N's reality, but the fact is everyone engages in role play to a degree in relationships. Co-dependents take a real person and act out a fantasy-romance in real life with him, while the N "borrows bodies" to act out a "virtual reality" fantasy in his mind. Other personality types "pretend" or imagine when they need to spice things up. Using fantasy in relationships can be healthy, but when fantasy becomes someone's "reality," it is considered a disorder and time to seek help.

Chapter 16

Troubled N Relationships

We know what sadness you are probably feeling. We empathize with you. It can be confusing and painful to examine one's life and relationships with honesty. In the process, it is often difficult to get a clear picture of what is "real." You may ask yourself questions like: "What *really* happened? Did I allow things to get *that* bad, or am I just over-reacting and being emotional?" Relationships are not black and white and it is in the "grey areas" that the N is a master of spin, deceit and manipulation. This, of course, adds to the confusion, which can lead to a general sense of powerlessness. We're going to look at two victims' experiences which we hope will help increase your understanding and insight into a few of the many confusing dynamics that can unfold in a relationship with Ns. As you read these experiences, pay attention to your intuition (a voice you may have ignored for far too long) and ask yourself to search for insights into similarities between these stories and your experiences.

Personal Relationships

Shauna and Mathew

Shauna's sound sleep was interrupted by the ringing of her telephone. She bolted upright and tried to gather her senses. The phone rang again. "Hello," she managed.

"Hey Babe," came the peppy voice on the other end of the line.

"What time is it?" Shauna squinted to see her alarm clock…two in the morning.

"Oh, I'm sorry," Mathew apologized. "I didn't realize how late it was. I couldn't sleep and I was thinking of you. I just needed to hear your voice."

Shauna's pulse quickened. So what if she had to get up in just a few hours? Mathew needed her.

Three hours later a groggy Shauna hung up the phone and rolled out of bed. Her job was going to be a challenge that day, but she at least felt as if she had been productive in working on her personal relationship. She and Mathew had been dating for eight months. They were talking about marriage but were trying to deepen their relationship before they committed to that step. Mathew had a lot going on in his life and his job was very stressful. According to Matthew, his ex-wife had never understood about his late hours and she had refused to let Mathew vent about his day. Shauna, on the other hand, understood how hard Mathew had to work and empathized with his unfortunate association with his inferior co-workers.

After listening to Mathew recount his long day and complain about his ex-wife, Shauna would start to discuss her own day. However, Mathew always would cut her off for one reason or another. This time was no different he said, "I'm sorry, Babe. I am fading fast. I really need to get some sleep if I am going to deal with those idiots at work tomorrow. I will call you tomorrow. Get some sleep. I love you. Goodnight." Months after their break-up, Shauna would realize that she never got to vent about her day.

For those of us with "N-awareness," Matthew's and Shauna's conversation actually translates like this:

I am not really sorry. I have just learned that it is appropriate to say, 'I am really tired' when I am being selfish and insensitive. I just needed to get some things off my chest. My day wasn't filled with enough narcissistic supply and I was feeling out of control. I needed to manipulate someone else's time for my own purposes in order to regain some of that much-needed control. It doesn't really bother me that I disturbed your sleep....after all, you are here to cater to me and to make me feel better...besides, you are doing me a service by listening to me and encouraging me. It is time well-spent. If I need you, I will grace you with another phone call sometime tomorrow...when it is convenient for me. Get some sleep...or don't. It doesn't really matter to me as long as you are available at my beck and call. I don't love you because I don't know how to love anyone. I don't even love myself. I only love my disorder. Goodnight.

The translation of the conversation may seem harsh, but the world of an N is not a pleasant place. Some N's are so sold into their disorder that they fool themselves into believing they are sensitive, caring people. However, what they perceive to be sensitivity is manipulation. An N may ask about his partner's day or about a sick relative as a courtesy or a lead into acquiring a favor from that person. If the person refuses to do the favor, the N will feel rejected and hurt. After all, how could someone be so insensitive as to refuse helping such a *caring, inquiring* person? The N's action of inquiring about another person is interpreted by the N as sensitivity, and he or she doesn't see it as a prelude or a "down payment" on a favor. Therefore, the N tricks himself into believing he has been offended and needs to seek supply for restitution.

Nick and Val

"*If she was so bad, why did you stay with her for so long?*" Nick's sister stared accusingly at him, waiting for an answer.

"*I can't explain it,*" Nick answered. "*No one would believe me if I tried.*"

"*Go ahead. Give it a shot,*" Courtney urged, pulling a lawn chair alongside him.

"*Well…*" Nick began, "*At first it was fun and exciting. She seemed to be everything I ever imagined. We had so much in common. I couldn't believe her first husband would walk away from such a dynamic young woman. Then I started to notice things that bugged me…little things at first. Her two kids from her first marriage could do no wrong, and if I ever tried to discipline them she shot me down…right in front of them. It was humiliating. I never saw her discipline them once; she had nothing but positive things to say about them.*"

"*So? Most mothers tend to brag about their kids,*" Courtney defended.

"*No…it was more than that. She seemed to have them placed on a pedestal. She would even tell them how much better they were than most people. They seemed to believe they were superior, as well. She and her children engaged in a lot of bashing other people…even perfect strangers. It was disgusting. Once I walked into the room and caught them bashing me.*"

"*Why didn't you mention any of this to me? This is the first time I've ever heard you say anything negative about Val. You two always seemed so happy when you came over. Her kids even seemed to like you in the beginning.*"

"*That was all an act…she had those kids trained to act the way she wanted them to act. When we were home, they acted differently… and so did their mother,*" Nick explained.

"*It's hard to believe all this,*" said Courtney.

"*I was afraid you'd say that. That's why I kept it all to myself.*" Nick was becoming frustrated. "*I knew you wouldn't believe it; I knew nobody would. That's why I never mentioned it to anyone. It seemed so bizarre that even I didn't believe it was happening at times!*"

"Calm down, I didn't say I didn't believe you; I said I found it hard to believe you. Val always seemed so pleasant. She was nice to everyone at our family gatherings, and she even seemed reluctant to tell us about your problem until we urged her. Finally, she broke down in tears and told us the whole story. And I want you to know that I don't feel any differently about you, Nick. You are my brother and I love you. The family has discussed it and we just want you to get better," Courtney patted her brother's shoulder and stared sympathetically into his eyes.

"My problem? And what problem is that?" Nick raged, pulling away from his sister.

"Now Nick, you must remain calm. It won't do any good if you get upset," Courtney looked scared and that frustrated Nick more.

"Why are you acting this way, Court? It's me...Nicky. Would I ever hurt you? I am angry because I have no idea what problem you're talking about! Until today, I assumed my only problem was getting mixed up with a crazy woman."

"Nick, Val told us about your control issues, and how you raged at her and the kids. She became afraid of you and that is when they began pulling away from you, too. She suspected that you were on some kind of drug because several pieces of her jewelry were missing and you were acting so strange. You raged at them for no particular reason. You seemed to go into bouts of depression. She encouraged you to see a doctor and he finally prescribed medication for schizophrenia for you. Nick, we know Uncle Thomas had problems with that and eventually had to be institutionalized. It runs in our family...it's genetic. It is nothing to be ashamed of. It's a disease...like cancer," Courtney stopped speaking and stood up. Nick's face had changed and his eyes were glowing with anger. Perhaps he had forgotten to take his medication. What if he didn't realize he was talking with his little sister and tried to hurt her?

Nick started toward her with balled fists at his sides. Then he turned and walked several paces away from her and lowered his head. When he had stood *there for several minutes Courtney's shaky voice broke the silence, "Nicky?"*

"I cannot believe that...that...woman. How could she make up such a horrible story about me? I let her move into my house with her bratty, unruly kids and tried to make a home for us. I put up with her ridicule, because I assumed that was her way of joking and that she hadn't really meant any of it. When she refused to let me discipline her kids, I told myself that since I wasn't their biological father, I had no right to discipline them...that maybe I could influence her in ways to do it so I wouldn't come across as being the 'bad guy.' I took a second job when she started spending more of my money. I just wanted her to be happy. When we were around other people, she was so friendly and loving. It reminded me of the way things were when we first got together. I didn't want anyone to know about her negative behavior because everyone seemed to like her. Everyone seemed to think I had finally done something right by picking a good woman. Besides, I knew she would change...I knew she would go back to the way she had been when we first met. Then no one would ever have to know how bad things had gotten. Everyone kept saying that we were meant for each other and that we were the role models for the perfect couple. I didn't want to let anyone down; I wanted to be a role model for the perfect couple. I was tired of being the poster boy for dysfunctional relationships. I thought with Val that I had a chance to have the dream." Tears were pouring from Nick's eyes and Courtney had relaxed a little, although she still appeared unsure of what he might do and kept her distance as he spoke.*

"Did I ever tell you that Val told me she was once pregnant with my baby?" Nick continued. "I was so excited. The thoughts of being a dad made me so happy I couldn't contain myself. I went out that first night after she had told me and bought all of this baby stuff...you know...like little bibs and ball caps. I even bought little pink hair bows. I really didn't care if it was a boy or a girl. I was going to be a daddy. Then several days later I noticed she was taking pills for menstrual cramps and I asked her about it. She said she was no longer pregnant and never talked about it again. Every time I tried to inquire about what had happened she became angry and raged at me. She was a totally different* person…it was scary, Court. I had never seen anything like it. She was worse than mom had been with us." Nick looked at his sister who walked a little closer to him. She stared wide-eyed into his face. Could it be that she had been wrong about Val this entire time?

"I don't have any proof of this, but I believe Val's miscarriage wasn't an accident. She mentioned several times how she didn't want to wreck her body with another pregnancy. She had spent so much money on tummy tucks and Yoga classes that it would be a waste to undo all she had accomplished. Besides, I heard her telling her kids once that she was afraid to dip into my gene pool. I think the thoughts of having my child disgusted her. After she lost the baby, I became depressed. If she hadn't wanted the child, she could have given him or her to me. I would have gladly taken my child and left her and her kids…on their own. The medication I am on is for depression, not schizophrenia. Now I am questioning whether I am in fact schizophrenic. Do you believe me?"

"I believe you believe yourself, and that's what matters." Courtney answered as if she were talking to a very young child.

"No, that's not all that matters, Court. Can't you see what is happening here? She has you convinced that I am the one with the problem. It's amazing to think that my own family would believe this stuff. I am the one who has been suffering in this relationship. I am the one who has had to deal with rage attacks and bizarre behavior. It was as if I were constantly walking on eggshells so I wouldn't set her off. I never knew what was going to cause her to flip out on me. One time I was supposed to stop by the wing place after work and bring some fried chicken home for dinner. That was the day that you called me and said that mom was upset and we needed to go over there."

"Yes, I remember. She'd had a car accident. She wasn't hurt, but needed us to come over right away."

"I know, but that was when I had to go over there and help you calm mom down. So I was late getting home and I forgot the fried chicken. Val was livid. You would have thought that I had left one of her kids by the side of the road somewhere. *She called me every name imaginable and raged for an hour. All the while her kids just looked on. Later that night she was acting all sweet as if nothing had ever happened, and wanted to take me to dinner. When I refused, she became really pouty and said that I had ruined it for her…that she couldn't enjoy herself now and that she would just make sandwiches for them at home. Of course, the kids had their hearts set on going out to eat and they became angry with me for spoiling their fun. Later, I heard them pleading with their mom to take them out without me. She said, 'You know how badly he makes me feel when he acts like that. I just don't want to go anymore. All I ever wanted was to have a happy home with a man who loved me and loved my children. But that is never going to happen. I have some sort of curse on me that causes me to hook up with the worst men in the world.' When she said things like that in the beginning of our relationship, I would feel bad for her and try to console her. I would buy her things and spoil her. Eventually, she would come around, but it wouldn't be long before I committed some other unforgivable act and I would be right back where I started. You have to believe me when I say that I have been living in torment for years with this woman."* Nick studied his sister's face, hoping for some sort of sign that she believed his account.

"But when you two were around the family, she seemed to be so attentive and caring toward you. And I remember one time you became moody; she just laughed and said, *'That's my Nicky. He can be a moody boy.'* We all felt a little sorry for her, because we knew that you could be moody at times." Courtney was having a hard time adjusting to the truth.

Nick understood Val put on a good act. It had never fooled him. He said, "I know it is hard to believe. I wouldn't believe me either…I covered up so much for so long. I tried to invent the perfect relationship. I wanted everyone to believe everything was great. I wanted to be the role model for a good relationship. I know I'm not perfect and I have my faults and I don't want to seem as if I am blaming her for everything that went wrong, but many of my actions were reactions to her crazy behavior." Nick knew that his sister wasn't totally convinced. The façade he had created of his relationship had been accepted. No one understood why he would stay in such a wacky situation. They had believed the false picture of serenity he had tried so hard to create and that his weird behavior had caused the only decent woman he had ever had to retreat from him. Nick looked hard at his sister hoping she would believe him. He needed somewhere to recover...somewhere he could get things together...grow strong again...get off his medication and get a job.

In fact, Nick had slowly become isolated from his friends and family. By confiding in his sister, Nick hoped to gain an ally, someone who could help him escape his disastrous situation. However, his sister wasn't sure who to believe. He had created more doubt in his sister's mind and had nowhere else to turn but to go back to Val. By doing this, he was perpetuating their sick relationship and when he got home, she had an angry tirade once again. Val acted as if she were the victim of the fender bender instead of Mom. Nick felt Val always had to be the center of attention, and if not, there would be hell to pay.

Marsha and Shanay

Marsha had just started her job at the ad agency when she first met Shanay. When Shanay came over to greet her, she was attracted and thought for sure that she felt something. She felt something more than just the cordial, "welcome-to-your-new-job" reception. Marsha felt that she had a keenly sensitive intuition when it came to sensing others who were gay. In fact, Marsha was confident in her intuitive powers in many areas of her life. She was proud that she had learned as a young woman that her "inner voice" was an important part of who she was. In the next few days, Marsha decided to suspend judgment on whether to try to establish a relationship. After all, she had always felt it was not a good thing to get involved with co-workers and still wasn't sure she should move ahead.

However, Shanay was the kind of woman who was difficult to "put on the back burner." She was a compelling presence: attractive, confident, creative, fun-loving and outgoing. Marsha noticed that Shanay had a special role in the company, and that she was very popular. Marsha concluded that Shanay was destined to be a star in the field of advertising. She could even picture herself working for Shanay one day, for Shanay seemed to have the charisma, the energy and the vision to go far. As time went on, Marsha learned to respect and admire Shanay, and though she tried to maintain a professional stance on the whole issue, she realized that she began to have feelings for Shanay. There was no denying it.

It came as no surprise to Marsha when Shanay was promoted, and gained a higher position than Marsha in a different department. Shanay was a natural leader who had no problem delegating tasks and managing her department with authority. Marsha noticed that Shanay had a very strong, assertive management style; in fact, it seemed that her assistants were actually rather in awe of her. Shanay met frequently with her assistants, and she had devised a wall chart system of accountability, where at a glance everyone could see who was performing at what level on what task. Shanay also implemented a new monthly evaluation program for her subordinates. Though she pushed her workers to their limits much of the time, and some complained of the long hours and workload, Shanay's department became famous for getting the job done ahead of schedule.

A few months later, Marsha and Shanay worked on a special joint project, requiring that they stay late at work and work at home on the weekends for several weeks. Their first romantic encounter was initiated by Shanay, and Marsha quickly reciprocated. Marsha was simply taken with Shanay's presence, strength and beauty. Shanay enjoyed Marsha's company, and told Marsha that she was a very special person who was like no one she'd ever met. Shanay opened up to Marsha and revealed things about her past she claimed to have never told anyone. Marsha felt Shanay trusted and valued her since Shanay was sharing such personal information about herself. Shanay kept saying how much she appreciated the fact that Marsha was a good listener.

At first, the things Shanay told her were very positive, but as Shanay began to discuss work more and more, Marsha was surprised to hear so many negative stories about the company and her co-workers. Nevertheless, Marsha felt Shanay certainly knew more than Marsha did about the politics of that particular office, and she was naturally curious to hear about Shanay's struggles at work. Shanay even talked about going out on her own one day to start her own advertising agency, because nobody appreciated her real worth, and so many people "held her back." Marsha was saddened to hear that Shanay was discouraged about her work situation, and she tried to encourage Shanay by telling her how incredible she was. Shanay said that when she struck out on her own to open her own ad agency, she would take Marsha with her, and they would be a team. They decided mutually, however, that their relationship should remain a secret for the time being.

It sometimes grew difficult for Marsha to keep their relationship under wraps. She had to ignore the desire to talk problems over with Shanay and they both had to act detached and disinterested. Shanay was very good at it and Marsha followed her lead. Sometimes Marsha felt a twinge of jealousy when Shanay went out to lunch each day with a different person from the office, especially when Marsha never got to be one of her lunch dates. Later when she brought it up, Shanay said she was being silly and changed the subject.

Marsha and Shanay spent so much time together after work that Marsha suggested they share an apartment. Shanay declined, saying that she needed to have her own place, but that they could spend lots of time together. They spent at least half of the week together after work, usually at Shanay's place, which was much nicer than Marsha's. Marsha often cooked for the two of them while Shanay stayed in her office at home talking on the phone or emailing clients, trying to tie up loose ends.

Not long after that, Shanay confronted Marsha about an ad campaign she was working on. Marsha felt confused and angry, for Shanay was not her direct boss, and Marsha felt she was doing a good job working within the budget and time frame allotted her. She had even gotten some positive feedback on the theme she'd created for the ad. Shanay, however, felt that Marsha had been taking too long, and that the ad was "tired" and "so 90's." To make matters worse, Shanay criticized Marsha in front of Marsha's team. She was not only hurt, but also found herself feeling worried that Shanay would not consider her "good enough" to go into business together when Shanay started her own agency. Nevertheless, Marsha maintained a professional demeanor in front of the team, and decided to talk to Shanay about it that night.

This was their first big fight. Marsha told Shanay that she felt hurt and embarrassed, and that the way she spoke to her was demeaning. She reminded Shanay that she was not her boss and had no right to criticize her work like that in front of Marsha's team. Shanay flew into an angry rage. Marsha was stunned. She lit into Marsha, yelling that if she couldn't take a little constructive criticism, she had no business being in advertising, and that she would never last as an ad executive because she was oversensitive. Shanay went on to say that Marsha was touchy like many others at the office who did not appreciate Shanay's superior skills, and that Shanay wished she could work at an agency where everyone could speak freely and offer input, and creativity would not be stifled with oversensitive people and stupid office politics! Shanay told Marsha that of all the people at work, she thought she could rely on Marsha to understand her. Then for the first time in their relationship, Marsha saw Shanay cry. Marsha was saddened to see this strong, dynamic person reduced to tears, and she felt responsible. Maybe she had been a little oversensitive. What was the big deal anyway about Shanay offering some input?

Marsha comforted Shanay and apologized. Then Shanay revealed a major drama unfolding at work, "I feel I am getting set up to be blamed for an ad campaign that went sour. You just didn't understand the pressure I'm under as an ad executive. I only hope you'll be ready for that level of stress, because someday I am going to start my own agency."

Marsha's feelings for Shanay grew, as did her dream to start their own ad agency. Marsha felt special, because she felt she was the only person who saw Shanay's vulnerable side, and she did her best to let Shanay know she could trust her, for she felt trust was a critical part of a good relationship. When Shanay opened up to her about her problems, she listened and tried to provide encouragement. Marsha felt this is what you do for the people you love. But when Shanay didn't extend that same support to her sometimes Marsha also felt down, and wished that Shanay could provide the same comfort that she offered Shanay. However, Shanay handled things differently. She either changed the subject after offering a quick comment or two, or made a joke to lighten the mood. Marsha decided that Shanay had too much on her mind and that she shouldn't burden her with her problems right now. Besides, Marsha was sure that if she had a big problem, Shanay would be there for her.

As time went on, Shanay "crossed boundaries" at work many more times by giving feedback or even confronting and criticizing Marsha. This often seemed awkward, because none of the other ad execs crossed team lines—they worked with their own team and no one else. Sometimes, Marsha acted as though Shanay had a good point; other times she stood her ground and defended her position, but she never brought it up at home, since it made Shanay angry, and any time she brought up the incidents, it would ruin their entire evening.

Marsha spoke frequently with her mother on the phone, and after several conversations about her relationship with Shanay, her mother finally revealed her true feelings about it: "It just seems that you're always the one giving, and she's always the one taking. And she is so mean to you sometimes! Does she really make you happy?"

Marsha assured her mom that Shanay was under a lot of pressure at work, and that they had a special relationship that she believed in. She told her mom that despite Shanay's tendency to make cold, cutting statements to people, she was actually a tender-hearted person underneath that hard exterior. Marsha explained, "You just have to get to know her."

"To be honest, honey, it seems like you're always making excuses for her," her mom said. Marsha asked her mom to give the relationship time. She felt a little irritated when her mom said, "Just be careful, honey."

However, Marsha's own patience was sorely tried and the trust in their relationship broke down when Marsha overheard some women from Shanay's team talking in the restroom. "So did you hear that Shanay might get transferred?" one of them said.

"Yeah, her team was complaining so much about her not pulling her weight that management is thinking of doing something about it. I heard that they had a talk with Shanay about it, and she actually tried to blame Marsha! She said that David, Marsha's ad exec, asked Shanay for assistance in motivating Marsha to do her job, and that she had spent so much time training her, it was taking time away from her own team."

Linda, one of Marsha's co-workers said, "Marsha does a really good job—I don't know what Shanay is talking about! Shanay is always stirring up trouble!"

"I know, but I heard that Shanay was 'rewarding' David, if you know what I mean, for backing her up on this. I don't know who is worse, David or Shanay!"

"David's just a dumb guy who can't turn down a hot woman. Shanay's a conniving, evil witch who backstabs everybody she comes in contact with. Poor David won't know what hit him when she's done using him."

"Poor David! What about Marsha!"

"Yeah, I wonder what will happen to Marsha. I suppose somebody should tell her."

"Not me! I'm staying out of it. Shanay's too dangerous."

"Did you hear what happened to Shanay at her last job? It began when she started going out with her boss, and she accused him of sexual harassment and got him fired. I heard that he was actually in love with her and had planned to propose. She was just using him...sleeping her way to the top, I hear."

"Just like she's been doing here."

"Exactly. So when he started getting serious, she became nasty and accused him of harassment. If you ask me, she was in control from the beginning. Once he was fired, Shanay got a big head, went on a power trip and everybody hated her. She eventually burned her bridges and had to leave, and I think that's what's happening here."

Marsha was devastated. She called her mother and told her what she'd heard. Her mom was very sympathetic and supportive, yet also very straightforward. "I never felt that she was a safe person, Marsha. I always wondered why your instincts didn't pick up on that—you're usually so good at reading people. It's like you gave yourself away to her, and she totally took advantage of you. I know it felt like love, but you must get out of that situation before it gets any worse."

Marsha knew that her mother was right, and she had some decisions to make. She decided to get her facts straight before confronting Shanay. In the meantime, she told Shanay that she had a lot of work to do and wouldn't be able to come over for awhile.

"Who's going to cook dinner?" Shanay asked. She seemed irritated about it, but eventually accepted Marsha's explanation.

The more digging Marsha did at work, the more she discovered Shanay's true nature. However, it was very dangerous because Shanay still had lots of admirers, and lots of power. Shanay was good at making things happen for people, because she knew it would make things happen for her. Whoever benefited from this at the time was extremely loyal to Shanay. Marsha had to be very careful because those who had to answer to Shanay were terrified of her.

As Marsha found out more about the way Shanay used and intimidated people, she began to see how she had been used and intimidated herself. She felt hurt, then angry—both at Shanay and at herself for not taking her time, and listening to her intuition. Marsha decided to invite Shanay over to confront her and end the relationship, but first she approached the president of the company to ask for a transfer to a different city. She knew she had to make a clean break to regain her dignity. The transfer was granted. Then Marsha met with Shanay. It was an explosive meeting. The more she confronted Shanay and told her how she felt, the more clearly she saw her try to manipulate, lie and play games to evade the confrontation. Shanay flew into a rage that was unlike anything Marsha had ever seen. Marsha felt frightened at the venom of Shanay's verbal attack. The rage was so powerful that Marsha worried Shanay might physically attack her.

Marsha finally ended the confrontation telling Shanay that she was moving to another city. She knew she would never forget the look in Shanay's eyes—a cold, demeaning look that made Marsha cringe. But she did not draw back. Marsha's clarity was coming back, and the more clearly she saw Shanay's dark side, the more Marsha realized how much Shanay had hurt her, and how much she needed time to heal. She decided that she needed to explore the experience and that time and reflection would help her use what she learned to grow and mature.

Maria and Juan

Maria leaned against her car window and inhaled deeply from her cigarette. How did everything get so messed up? Looking back over the past few months, Maria was amazed that she let herself become involved in certain activities. Juan had such a magical effect on her. She knew she couldn't blame him, though. She was a grown woman who made her own choices. She certainly could have refused. However, she wanted to please Juan more than she had ever wanted to please any other man. Things he had suggested they explore in the bedroom were things she would have found appalling before she met him. But Juan made her feel so comfortable and loved. She trusted him more than she had trusted any other partner. Unfortunately, Juan abused that trust and she found herself in shock for being so blind.

Maria found Juan's insatiable sexual appetite a turn-on in the beginning *of their relationship. He never seemed to tire of her sexually. They would have sex five or six times a day. Eventually, Juan started adding things to their sex lives to "spice things up." At first, Maria was apprehensive about experimenting in such ways, but Juan made her feel so at ease and comfortable that she found herself acting out things she never imagined doing. Still, nothing seemed to satisfy Juan. The more they experimented, the more Juan wanted to do. One day he asked Maria if she would invite one of her girlfriends over to join them in bed. Maria was heartbroken. She considered all the experimentations to be sacred to their relationship. She felt that by crossing certain lines in the bedroom, she was gaining Juan's trust and solidifying their relationship. Suddenly she felt used. Juan saw her as a plaything...an object...a willing object.*

Around others, Juan seemed so normal. No one would have guessed that he had this private life. He was very active in his community and involved with charity events. He always seemed to have the perfect thing to say at public gatherings. Initially, Maria prided herself on being so special to Juan because he let her sneak a peek into his very private side. The charming, charitable man of the public was obviously the real Juan. Maria got to see the private Juan...the one he reserved only for her, because they were so close and he had come to trust her so much.

That is why it was so devastating for Maria when she learned that Juan's sexual appetite wasn't only being satisfied with her...and that he had been lying about his many lady "friends." Maria felt used and stupid. She had thought herself to be too old and too intelligent to fall for such games. She had really convinced herself that her relationship was an exclusive, special relationship that had evolved into a deep bond of trust...and it was...for her.

Maria couldn't believe that Juan had slept with other partners while still in a relationship with her. Had he been engaging in those perverted acts with his other partners as well? What Maria didn't realize was that Juan's twisted sexual desires were much more than sexual deviancy. Juan was a Somatic Narcissist. His sexual attitude was a result of that.

According to Dr. Sam Vaknin, author of *Malignant Self-Love: Narcissism Revisited*, somatic narcissists often resort to sex when they aren't getting enough adoration or attention intellectually. Dr. Vaknin explains that somatic narcissists use sex as a tool to boost the number of sources of narcissistic supply. He states that if sex is the most efficient weapon in the narcissist's arsenal—he or she becomes reckless with it.

Basically, if the narcissist can't acquire admiration, adoration, or any other type of positive recognition for intellect—he or she chooses sex as an alternate means of gaining approval. Vaknin explains that the narcissist becomes a satyr (or a nymphomaniac), who will haphazardly have sex with many different partners. He or she considers their sex partners as objects—sources of Narcissistic Supply. Through seduction and sexual conquest the narcissist obtains his or her desperate craving for a narcissistic "fix." A narcissist will often perfect his method of flirtation and consider his or her sexual exploits as artwork. The Narcissist generally reveals this side—without inhibition—to others, and anticipates to gain their admiration and support. Because the Narcissistic Supply (in a narcissist's situation) is a matter of defeat and believed inferiority—the narcissist has no choice but to constantly leap from partner to partner.

Of course, there are normal couples who engage in sexual fantasy during their relationships. That doesn't automatically qualify one as a Somatic Narcissist. In Juan's case, however, his insatiable sexual urges, multiple partners, constant lies, and smooth-talking attitude were only a few characteristics that distinguished him from "normal."

When Maria confronted Juan about his other partners and expressed her shock and dismay over his inability to be satisfied with her alone, he became manic and raged at her. He accused her of being overly dramatic and closed-minded. He informed her that there were plenty of other women who would appreciate him and that someone of her caliber was very lucky to have someone like him even remotely interested in her. He reminded her that he had been with beautiful, successful women before she came along, and that he could have more any time he wished. He said he hadn't wanted to tell her this in the beginning of their relationship, but initially he felt sorry for her. She had been a wreck. No decent man would have wasted any time on her.

As Maria sat in her car, smoking one cigarette after another, she recounted all the horrible things Juan had said to her before he walked out. He seemed to just move on with his life, giving no thought to the months they had spent together. They had been talking about moving in together and although Juan had yet to introduce her to his family, she was looking forward to being a part of their lives eventually. She didn't understand why he lied to her about feeling sorry for her in the beginning of their relationship. She remembered how he had showered her with attention and compliments. He never stopped talking about how she was the epitome of the perfect woman and that he had finally met his match. He seemed so convincing. Was he lying? He couldn't have been, because he seemed so sincere. The way he seemed to rush things and need her had been a red flag for Maria, but she found herself going along with everything as Juan eventually convinced her that they were soul mates.

Months into their relationship they began arguing a lot, but the make-up sex was great. Juan had a lot of issues with a controlling father who had not provided him with much love and affection, so naturally he had some intimacy issues; but Maria thought they were conquering those problems, because they seemed to be growing closer physically.

Nothing made sense anymore. Maybe Juan was right. Maybe she was overbearing and closed-minded. What if he had rescued her from a life of solitude? What if she weren't good enough for any decent man? Had she messed up the one good thing that came along? Maria began to feel guilty and stupid. She thought about the fun she and Juan used to have...their crazy adventures...the way he would text her or email her during the day. She felt crushed when Juan didn't write to her. Later, he called or emailed as if he hadn't skipped contact for a couple of days. She got upset that he hadn't at least called. Then Juan became *upset, because she was so needy. She hadn't always been needy. When had that happened? She pulled the visor down and glanced at herself in the mirror. Where was that happy, independent woman?*

Narcissistic Parents

Does Narcissism breed Narcissism?

Ideally, it would be comforting to think that we're not entirely shaped by our parents. It would be encouraging to believe that environment and the influence of those closest to us has only a minor impact on the individuals we become.

However, of course our parents mold us to an extent. As children we're so easily affected by those who claim they love us. The question remains as to whether the love is a selfish love or a boundless love.

Generally, narcissistic parents are inclined to have children of their own to fulfill selfish needs. The parent sees their child as an extension of themselves. As seen through the eyes of a Narcissist, a child provides immortality. Because of this distorted perspective, the Narcissistic parent has to exert extreme control over his/her child, who in turn has no choice but to comply.

Naturally, this control is generated via several methods: the guilt trip, the idea that the parent is dependent on the child, the concept that the parent and child share the same goal and threats to the child if he/she does not adhere to these rules. By using these techniques, the Narcissist is able to constantly remind him/herself that the child is a part of him/her. Needless to say, this thought process leads to an emotionally unstable relationship between parent and child. The narcissistic parent views his/her children as Secondary Narcissistic Supply. A young child will allow the narcissistic parent to obtain everything he/she desires: unconditional love, admiration and obedience. When the child is no longer willing or able to grant his/her parent this attention, the parent may react in an insensitive manner. At this point, the crux of the irrational relationship is revealed. The Narcissist responds with various forms of aggression: disdain, anger, and emotional or physical abuse.

The domino effect persists. The children of Narcissists will ultimately end up becoming involved in a narcissistic relationship (in which they act as co-dependents), or they themselves evolve into Narcissists as a result of their detrimental upbringing.

In the case of Wayne and his father, Wayne's father proves to be a typical narcissistic parent who endlessly continues to attempt control over his son's life.

Wayne and His Father

Wayne's son went on vacation without telling his father where he was going. Because Wayne's father was an N, he was very controlling and needed to know Wayne's whereabouts at all times. When he learned that Wayne had left without informing him of the wheres, whens and hows of his vacation, Wayne's father became enraged. He told everyone he spoke with about what an insensitive son Wayne was. He ranted about Wayne's irresponsibility to anyone who would listen. As people listened to his angry words, Wayne's father gained narcissistic supply. This helped him gain back some of the control he felt he lost when Wayne didn't inform him of his whereabouts. Narcissistic parents need to feel as if they are in charge of their children's lives even when their children become adults.

Vivian

Vivian's poor health prevented her from leaving her house, but when her children choose to pay her visits, she chastised them. Vivian complained about how they didn't care enough about her to call often or see her enough. She made it very difficult for anyone to repeat a visit. Since she criticized their appearance and picked on them for not meeting her expectations, they wished they never had come. Vivian didn't realize that she made everyone's visit a negative experience. She assumed that regardless of her topics and disposition, her children should feel obligated to visit her. Most of her conversations were about her poor health, her poor choices in life, or people in her life that had disappointed her. As the children avoided Vivian more frequently, she became more and more bitter. Of course, in Vivian's mind the world was an evil place overall so it was no wonder her children continued to disappoint her. Because Ns are not aware of their flaws, as they age they become more moody and unpleasant, they do not notice how miserable they can make others feel...nor do they seem to care.

Alyssa and Scott

Alyssa and Scott were married as soon as she finished her senior year in college. Earlier, she had other boyfriends, but Scott was her first long-term, serious relationship. Months after their wedding, Scott became clingy. Each time Alyssa went into another room, Scott followed her and asked what she was doing. Alyssa felt as if she had no privacy. In the evenings, when Alyssa sat on the couch to watch television, Scott sat right next to her. Sometimes he began rubbing her leg or kissing her neck. After a while, Alyssa began to feel smothered. One day, she found Scott checking her email. They had given each other their email passwords, but Alyssa had never checked Scott's email. When Scott's friends called, Alyssa left the room to give him privacy. But if any of Alyssa's friends called, Scott sat next to her and pouted until she got off the phone. Later, Scott made comments such as, "I don't know why your friends have to call you all the time. Don't they know you have a life?" When Alyssa reminded him that his own friends called him more often than her friends called her, he continued to argue and pout.

When they'd been married five years, Alyssa decided to go back to school to get her Master's Degree. She was excited about her decision, because she knew it meant more money and she was looking forward to furthering her career. Scott became apprehensive about her decision. He complained about how much money it would cost for her to go back to school and reminded her that they were planning to have a baby. What kind of a mother would be so selfish as to put her career before her own child? She needed to stay home and raise their children. Besides, he made enough money for both of them and he only had a Bachelor's Degree. Why did she feel the need to get a higher degree anyway? Was she trying to make him feel inferior?

No matter how much Alyssa tried to explain, Scott refused to see her viewpoint. He accused her of being a selfish person and told her that she couldn't possibly love him as much as he loved her.

Alyssa accused Scott of being a control freak who was used to getting his way with his mother and expected his wife to continue the same pattern. She said, "You can go and buy an expensive bike, yet you don't want me to go back to school." Scott would then turn the argument around and say, "If you don't want me to keep the bike I will sell it." He accused Alyssa of being a lesbian, because she rarely wanted to have sex with him. Alyssa explained, "Who wants to have sex with someone who doesn't even trust her? You check my email and my voice mail all the time. I don't know what you are expecting to find. I am faithful to you and I always have been. Yet, you don't even want me to go out with my friends to have a drink after work. You know I never drink more than one drink...but you still complain if I go with them. Even when I promised you I wouldn't drink with them, you still called them my 'drinking buddies' and put them down. You make me feel ashamed of my friends and they are good people. I don't know why you are always insulting my friends. Your friends are not perfect, yet you never hear me putting them down. I can never do anything right in your eyes."

Of course, after that type of confrontation, Scott always put on his best behavior. He sent Alyssa sweet text messages and emails. He took her out to her favorite restaurant and made huge efforts to be pleasant...not saying anything negative about her family or friends.

As soon as Alyssa became comfortable again, Scott continued his controlling behavior. Alyssa always felt inferior in intelligence to Scott, because his test scores were always higher than hers in college...and he always made an effort to point that out to her. In fact, any time Alyssa made a mistake, Scott was quick to point it out. He would sometimes do it as if he were joking, but Alyssa knew he was trying to hurt her. She never understood why he wanted to hurt her. She tried to lift him up and encourage him as much as possible. When he made a mistake, Alyssa would try to make him feel better by explaining that it was no big deal or a mistake that anyone could have made.

One night, after Alyssa answered a phone call from a friend, Scott once again began to pout and treat Alyssa with a negative attitude. Finally Alyssa said, "I wish you wouldn't get so upset when my friends call. Most of my friends have stopped telephoning me, because they know how critical you are about it, but I enjoy hearing from them now and then." Scott replied, "Well, at least someone calls you. Your own parents practically ignore you." Alyssa couldn't believe Scott needled her by mentioning that her parents rarely called. His parents checked in on a daily basis, but Alyssa wasn't as close to her own parents. Besides, it was long distance for her parents to call and Scott's parents lived down the street.

Finally, Alyssa felt she could no longer take the controlling abuse Scott was giving her. She told him she wanted to separate from him. Scott began to cry and tell Alyssa how much she meant to him. He told her that he knew he could be controlling at times, but that he was going to work on it. He said the only reason he came across so strongly was because he loved her so much and that he felt as if she were slipping away from him. He said, "You used to like to be kissed by me. We snuggled on the couch and did everything together. Now you act as if you don't even want to be around me. We rarely ever talk any more."

Alyssa said, "We used to see each other only on the weekends and we talked about what we did all week. Now we are with each other all the time and we know what we do all week. Besides, when I try to tell you about work you *complain that you don't want to hear about it all the time. Yet, you will vent about your workday for hours. I told you the reason I don't feel like snuggling and kissing all the time. You are constantly checking my email and my cell phone, you hate when my friends call and you don't like it when my family comes to visit. Yet, you make sure you get little digs in when they don't visit. I feel like a prisoner in my own home. If I go into the other room to fold laundry, your feelings get hurt because I am not folding it in the same room with you. You think I am trying to escape you all the time. You make me feel so stressed and uncomfortable."*

Scott began to cry and sulk again. *"I cannot believe you feel that way. I'm the victim here, not you. You only see your side of the situation and you're too selfish to see my side. You don't even realize how much you've changed since we got married. You have pulled away and have become distant. When I try to kiss you I feel you tense or pull away. You act as if I want you to cut off your right arm when I want to have sex and then you just lie there like a rag doll until it is over. You make me feel badly about myself. I try to do everything to make you happy. I send you nice emails and romantic text messages. I plan elegant dinners for you and walk on eggshells so I won't upset you or set you off. Nothing I do is good enough for you."*

Realizing that their relationship was failing, the couple decided to go to a marriage counselor. It turned out to be a disaster. Scott became angry when the therapist suggested that he needed to back off and give Alyssa some space. But realizing that the therapist may have perceived his attitude as negative, Scott calmed down and admitted that he could be a bit controlling at times. He promised that he would start making an effort to be more understanding.

Several days after the first visit to the marriage counselor, Scott made an effort to treat Alyssa more respectfully. However, Alyssa felt that Scott was trying so hard to be nice that it didn't seem sincere. Watching his face and body language, she could tell that there were times when Scott seemed ready to explode.

Before long, Scott was back to his old critical behavior, dictating to Alyssa and complaining about her friends and family. Following their usual pattern, Alyssa recoiled and drew away from him and Scott became angrier and fault finding.

Had Scott continued counseling it probably would have revealed that he suffered from Narcissistic Personality Disorder. His need to control Alyssa is a classic narcissistic trait. Slowly eliminating close friends and family from their partner's life is another common trait among N's. By constantly ridiculing Alyssa's friends, Scott made sure Alyssa began refusing their phone calls. He made negative comments about Alyssa's parents, comparing them to his parents, hoping Alyssa would see them as inferior or uncaring, thus making it easier for her to cut ties with them.

Scott's fear of Alyssa's success caused him to strike out against her decision to return to college and obtain her Master's Degree. An N has a deep fear of abandonment and if his partner becomes too self-sufficient she will no longer depend upon him, making it more likely that she could walk away. Ns like to keep their supply dependent upon them in every way. By continuing to insult Alyssa's intelligence, Scott chipped away at Alyssa's self-esteem, making her more dependent upon his masterful mind. However, Scott feared Alyssa's eventual recognition of his inferior true self and he knew that would send her packing.

His own negative attitude toward himself caused him to project his negative traits and insecurities upon Alyssa. He projected his insecurities about his low intelligence onto Alyssa, convincing her that she was inferior to him. His less-than-desirable relationship with his own parents caused him to convince Alyssa that her parents didn't care for her. Even though his parents were constantly visiting and calling, Scott knew it to be more of a control issue rather than care. Yet, he referred to it as care in order to strike out at Alyssa and convey her parents fell short of being ideal parents.

Scott wanted to have children with Alyssa to gain more control over her. He could use the guilt card where the children's care was concerned and thus Alyssa would do what he wanted. An N's children are objects to him. If they can be used to help him gain supply, then they have served their purpose.

Whenever Alyssa reacted against his possesiveness and began to fight with Scott, Scott felt threatened and his fear of abandonment surfaced. His defense mechanisms kicked in and he tried everything in his power to keep her from leaving. The reason Scott seemed insincere when he treated Alyssa kindly, was because he was insincere. He was desperate and acting out in ways that seemed to work in the past. This type of learned behavior is similar to the behavior modification therapists teach N's to help them with their relationships. The N's never feel sincere when they act in those selfless, amiable ways. They are just acting out a scene that usually gets them what they want.

When Scott cried or pouted to get his way, he was more than likely using techniques that had worked for him with his mother when he was younger. Those actions were used to obtain narcissist supply and usually worked for him. He didn't really feel wounded or hurt…he felt threatened. He felt as if he were going to lose his supply, or worse, his control. New supply can always be obtained, but that lack of control is unbearable to an N.

An ironic twist to this case is that had Alyssa been less independent…had she wanted Scott to snuggle and kiss her…had she not wanted to have private phone calls or time alone away from him, Scott would have found her to be weak. Weakness is undesirable to an N. He would have probably crushed her self-esteem and eventually moved on to stronger, more-confident supply.

Ironically, Alyssa's poise and independence is what kept her N clinging onto to her.

Blaming the Victim

Yun-Jin and Samir

Yun-Jin (Jinny)'s friends and relatives wondered what happened to Jinny after her marriage to Samir. "She used to be so outgoing and confident. Now she seems to stay in her house with the blinds drawn, alienating herself from all of her friends. I hardly hear her laugh anymore. She's not the same person."

Jinny, being the classic co-dependent, felt the need to put on a show for everyone. In other words, she would cover for Samir every chance she got. Samir's addiction to alcohol dictated his attitude. Sometimes he was a fun-loving goof, other times he was angry and downright mean. As the months passed and Jinny saw the cycle repeating itself, she became withdrawn and depressed. But like a good little co-dependent, Jinny "kept up appearances" when she was around others, especially family members.

At family get-togethers, Samir often treated Jinny with more respect. In the beginning of their relationship Jinny would buy into it, but it didn't take long before she realized it was just an act for other people. Once they were back in the "safety" of their own home, Samir resorted to being neglectful or verbally abusive. Jinny kept their blinds drawn and stayed inside most of the time. Subconsciously she felt as if she were hiding an ugly truth. She didn't want anyone learning the reality of her situation. Besides, Samir constantly promised to change and be more attentive and less insulting. Jinny felt that most of his actions were due to his alcoholism and that it wasn't his fault. She felt sorry for him and knew that she had married him for better or worse and wasn't about to leave him when the chips were down. She truly believed he would get it together eventually and treat her the way she deserved to be treated. In the meantime there was no need to reveal the truth to anyone else. When things got better, and they would, there would be no reason for anyone to know their relationship hadn't always been great.

Samir decided to leave when depression got the better of him. Jinny felt devastated because she had waited so long for him to change and treat her with more respect. Five years of her life were lost and she couldn't get them back. Jinny convinced Samir to see a therapist with her. She didn't want to lose the time they had together. After a few sessions with the therapist Jinny was feeling as if things were improving. Samir even mentioned that he was noticing a change and feeling more positive about things. Two days after their last session with the therapist, Samir disappeared. Jinny was confused; she had thought things were going well. Samir said that he was feeling better about their relationship. How could he say those things and then leave?

N's say what they think they are expected to say. As long as they feel they can gain supply from someone, they will try to be on their best behavior. However, if they feel there is nothing to be gained, N's will say what they feel...regardless of how rude it comes across. By relocating, Samir had a chance to erase his previous life and start fresh in a new location. Jinny often wondered if Samir missed her or thought about their life together.

Samir simply left and never looked back. Samir never mentioned Jinny again unless someone brought her up...and then Samir said only what people expected him to say about her. Jinny, on the other hand, had to deal with family members who had no clue things had been as bad as they were for her. Because of her appealing façade, Jinny convinced those around her that her marriage was nearly perfect. Her lies and cover-ups came back to haunt her when she tried to explain Samir's abusive behavior. Co-dependents do such a wonderful job of covering for their partners that it becomes difficult to convince anyone of the truth. On the other hand, Samir didn't have explaining to do. He simply moved on and started fresh without baggage. That cut and dry attitude is hard for most people to understand. But the "normal" emotions that enable people to feel regret or empathy are destroyed early in the splitting of the N's life. He is not capable of those types of feelings, and while that is unfortunate, it is also unfair to project them onto him.

Victims of N's rarely gain closure from their N after their relationship ends. An N is able to disconnect and move onto another relationship without looking back at his previous one. The victim wants the N to

admit some wrongdoing on his part and apologize for any pain he may
have caused. That is not likely to happen.

Some victims create their own form of closure by acting out
break-up scenes either with a friend, therapist or in their minds or by
writing their feelings down. Chances are if the letter is sent the N won't
read it, but the victim gains that closure and is able to move on.

Dana, one victim to whom we spoke, suggested that there be a
support group called PAN (People against N's). She went on to explain
that the word "PAN" could also represent Peter Pan and how he never
grew up.

N's tend to live in their fantasy worlds of false self, acting selfishly
as a child would. While there is no group that calls itself "PAN," there
are many support groups online for victims of narcissistic abuse, such as
the msn.com website group called "N Partners," nonbpd.org and
Healthyplace.com (which provides various links to other resources for
coping with narcissism). If you have been victimized, realizing that you
are not alone and gaining support from others who've been through
similar situations can be comforting.

Rhoda and Dan

*We spoke to Rhoda, a woman in her late thirties. She had recently been
divorced from her first husband of twenty-one years and began a frantic pursuit
of a new mate. Rhoda felt like a failure, because she was divorced. Never mind
the fact that her husband had ignored her throughout their entire marriage. He
cared more about the Internet than he did about her. He sat in front of his computer for hours and promised her he would "be off in a minute," but in fact
rarely paid any attention to her. It angered her to think of all of the broken
promises and the lost moments. Rhoda had practically raised their daughter by
herself. Rhoda had watched as her daughter began to receive the same treatment*

from her father. At the computer he would say, "Daddy will be off in a minute. I will take you four-wheeling after a while."

Broken promises and broken dreams were all Rhoda had left from her twenty-one-year marriage. She was determined to get it right the next time. She would marry someone the exact opposite of her first husband and she would demand all of his time. For once in her life, someone was going to pay attention to her. No more missed birthdays and empty promises. Her next husband was going to treat her like a queen.

Unfortunately, her inability to stand being alone as a single parent fueled her desire to quickly land a husband. This is what caused Rhoda to end up with Dan the Man. Dan was a few years younger than Rhoda and he loved to party. He hated computers and knew nothing about them. Rhoda felt as if she had hit the jackpot. The first few months of their relationship were ideal. Dan complimented Rhoda constantly. Never before had Rhoda had so much in common with one person. They loved each other's company. Dan explained to her that his two ex-wives had been so different from Rhoda. They had not understood him. They didn't like to party and they ended up being such nags. Rhoda prided herself on her heightened insight and her ability to enjoy a good time. She and Dan danced until the wee hours of the morning. She woke up with hangovers on numerous occasions. Rhoda had not partied so much since college. But, her daughter was a teenager and this was Rhoda's time to enjoy life. She had led such a miserable existence during her marriage that she had forgotten what it was like to have fun. Never again would someone keep her from enjoying herself. She was tired of always giving and never receiving. She had met the man of her dreams and they had fallen in love. She couldn't get over how much they had in common. It was like a fairy tale. Dan begged her to get her tubes untied and give him a baby. His first two wives hadn't been able to conceive and he loved Rhoda so much that he wanted a child from her. Rhoda took that as the purest form of flattery. Her only child was about to start college and she had assumed her baby-

rearing days were over. But here was this man…this man that loved her so much that he wanted to have a child with her. Rhoda consented and five months later she was pregnant with Dan's baby. They were married and spent a quick honeymoon in Vegas. Rhoda had to stop partying because of the pregnancy, but Dan didn't let up at all. He celebrated the pregnancy, the marriage, life, love, the sun and the stars. There was always an excuse for a party.

At first, Rhoda didn't notice how drinking beer and smoking pot seemed to be the focus of their relationship. She had been so caught up in new love that she hadn't noticed anything else. But after she became pregnant, she urged Dan to slow down and take things more seriously. She began to wonder if he wanted his child to grow up seeing his or her father drunk or high all of the time. The time had come for Dan to ease up on the bad habits and look for a steady job. Dan didn't have a college degree and usually kept himself busy with part-time jobs, delivering pizza or working at the car wash. His jobs never lasted more than three months. No one seemed to understand him. No one "got him." The fact of the matter was that Dan found it difficult to get up early enough each morning to hold a steady job. He spent most days until late in the afternoon sleeping off his hangover. Then he would rise, eat something cold from the fridge and head to the beach. Some of Dan's party-buddies would meet him at the beach to play Frisbee golf. Sometimes Dan would just sleep all day. Rhoda found herself growing frustrated with Dan's lack of enthusiasm over the baby, their marriage, finding a job and anything that didn't involve partying.

It was then that Rhoda began to re-evaluate their relationship. It had all been a blur of partying and lovemaking. It had all seemed so romantic and carefree in the beginning. But Dan had gotten more into the drugs and alcohol as time progressed. Eventually, it wasn't much of a fairy tale. Rhoda learned from Dan's parents that he had been in and out of rehab several times. Now she knew he had a serious problem with all types of drugs and that was the real reason he had lost two wives to divorce. She wished she had that information in the beginning of their relationship. But she was truthful with herself. Since she had been so caught up in having fun, would it have mattered?

Rhoda had so wanted to "get it right this time" that she may have convinced herself that she could change Dan. She may have thought that she could "cure him," or that his love for her was so great that he would finally overcome anything negative in his life. After all, they had so much in common.

Rhoda and Dan's daughter was born with heart disease and was in need of several operations. Rhoda blamed herself for having her tubes untied in her late thirties. Her conscience gnawed away at her for partying so much before the pregnancy. In addition, she knew that birth defects could be linked to the father and Dan had not ceased to drink alcohol and smoke weed before the conception of their daughter. Their daughter's operations were expensive and Dan didn't have insurance since he only worked part-time at the Pizza Hut. Eventually, the stress became overwhelming for Dan. He and Rhoda argued all the time. Rhoda felt angry that Dan didn't seem to care for their daughter the way she did.

Anger grew within her and Rhoda began lashing out at Dan. She couldn't understand why he was content with his part-time, meaningless jobs. She didn't know why it didn't bother Dan that his daughter was going to grow up watching her daddy get drunk and quit jobs all the time. Dan accused Rhoda of nagging him every day. He said she had changed. She wasn't the same woman he had married. His friends had warned him about her. She was too good to be true.

"Women lure you in with their carefree attitude and then, once they have you, they expect you to straighten up and change your entire life. Well, I am the same way I was when I met her and if she hadn't liked me she shouldn't have married me," Dan rationalized.

Rhoda tried to convince him that her change in attitude had everything to do with their daughter. She wanted to act more responsibly for their daughter. Rhoda had enjoyed the partying for a time…but she didn't expect to do it for-

ever. People had to grow up and act responsibly, eventually. The partying was fun and romantic and an escape from her depression over her divorce, but eventually things had to settle down and they had to live a mature life, especially since they were now parents of a special needs child.

One day Rhoda awoke to find Dan gone. He had not left a note, but his clothes were missing from their closet. For weeks, Rhoda never heard from him. She was devastated. While she was at the hospital visiting her daughter who'd had another operation, Rhoda received a call on her cell phone. It was Dan. He said he had left because he couldn't take the stress anymore. Things had been great when they were first together, but Rhoda had changed and had become a nag like his ex-wives and his mother. She wasn't the same fun-loving party-woman she had been when he met her. He had misjudged her. She would be receiving divorce papers from him in the mail.

Rhoda asked what he intended to do about their daughter. She knew he wouldn't be able to hold down a job long enough to send any child support. Besides, any money he did make would be spent on booze and drugs. Dan said he was thirty years old and half his life was over. He said he really wanted to find happiness before he got too old to enjoy life. He said Rhoda should raise their daughter alone, because as Rhoda had told him, he wouldn't be a good influence on her, anyway.

His words made Rhoda feel guilty. What if she had driven him away with her accusations that he wasn't a good father? She knew Dan loved their daughter. He had held her many times and even changed her diaper. He always seemed so proud of her when he talked about her to anyone. He carried her picture in his wallet and showed everyone he met. "She's got my nose," he boasted. Perhaps Rhoda had been too hard on him... After all, he had been in and out of rehabilitation and wasn't as emotionally strong as most people. How could she expect him to be as responsible as other men when he had suffered so much for so long? Besides, Dan was right...he was the same when she met him...she was the one that had changed. She reminded Dan of the good times they had shared...the parties they had attended together...their walks on the beach. Before she had hung up the phone, Rhoda had convinced Dan that they should give their marriage another chance.

A few days later Dan called Rhoda and said, "I've been thinking...I don't mind trying to get back together, but I am really not ready to be a father. I thought I could do it...but it is just not for me. I would be a bad influence on her, anyway. She needs to be around someone who will be good for her and raise her in a way that I am not capable. If you still want to get back together with me you need to see if your mom will take care of our daughter, because I really can't handle that right now."

Rhoda was devastated. She couldn't believe Dan was suggesting that they give their daughter to her mother to raise. Rhoda hung up the phone and cried. Why was she always getting stuck with the jerks in life? Was she some sort of jerk magnet? All she wanted was to have a good marriage and to have someone love her and pay attention to her. Was that so much to ask? She loved her tiny, sick daughter, but realized without a partner caring for her child would be difficult, yet knew that's what she had to do. Nevertheless, she resented Dan for convincing her to have a child and then deserting her.

Though all of that seemed very unforgivable, Rhoda found herself missing Dan uncontrollably. She missed the way he had made her feel in the beginning of their relationship before she became pregnant. No one had ever made her feel that way. He had been her best friend. They were so much alike. She had never enjoyed anyone's company as much as she did Dan's. She missed his touch. Her first husband had never been able to make her feel the way Dan had in bed.

She cried all the time and didn't eat. How could he just erase her and their daughter from his memory that way? It was as if he just picked up with another life and began fresh...trying to have fun before his life ended. And what about her? Rhoda's feelings of longing were mixed with bouts of confusion and anger. None of it made sense to her, yet she found herself wanting to go to Dan and start fresh. She even began to think of leaving their daughter with her mom until *she could convince Dan to settle down and take things more seriously. Maybe, if she partied with him like the old days, he would be happier and he would realize that there weren't many women who could have as much fun with him and understand him the way she did. Once he remembered how special she was, Dan would be willing to follow her to the ends of the earth. Then she could convince him that he would be a good influence on their daughter, after all. Back and forth, her thoughts flew.*

Rhoda had subconsciously chosen a man very much like her first husband. Like him, Dan cared only about himself. Rhoda's first husband ignored her as he catered to his own desires, leaving Rhoda feeling alone and frustrated. Convinced that she would be involved with her next husband's hobbies, Rhoda found herself mixed up in a world of drugs and alcohol. She told herself it was the "honeymoon phase" of her new relationship and that that sort of behavior couldn't last forever. What she didn't realize was that she had entered the stage of her N's play. He wrote the script and it didn't involve his co-star changing his rules. As long as she had been willing to enable him, Rhoda was allowed to stay. But as soon as she began changing the script, it was time to write her out of the play. N's rarely make loving, selfless parents so Dan's attitude toward his daughter wasn't surprising. She was an object to him, and was discarded when she was no longer wanted.

Rhoda's codependency caused her to consider giving up her own daughter in order to revive what she considered to be an ideal relationship. What she didn't realize was that she had been idealized in the beginning and then eventually discarded. Rhoda had been convinced of the false image Dan had created of her. She wanted to be that understanding, insightful, ideal love. She wanted to be the one that made his dreams finally come true. He made her feel so special. To believe that she had been discarded meant realizing that she hadn't been special at all. Rhoda wasn't ready to accept that. She had convinced herself that she had been so much better for Dan than his first two wives. No one understood him the way she had. She couldn't fathom all the things they had in common as anything but an uncanny coincidence. She wasn't ready to let anyone take that away from her. She was willing to do whatever it took to get her partner back. She had seen a good side of him in the beginning of their relationship. She was going to do whatever it took to bring that side of him back again. By being willing to follow him to the ends of the earth, Rhoda was showing her vulnerability...her dependence or her neediness for Dan. What she didn't realize was that those qualities would eventually cause her to self destruct.

Dan had severed his supply once he left his family. His parents were disappointed in him for abandoning his wife and child; Rhoda's parents were convinced more than ever of his inabi lity to provide for their daughter. His friends helped Rhoda search for him during his absence, fearing that he may have passed out near the beach and drowned. Once everyone realized what had actually occurred, any positive opinions of Dan were erased. Dan had no choice but to relocate. Once an N's supply has been depleted, he must move on and find a new companion.

Chapter 17

N's and the Internet

Many N's spend their lives moving from place to place and person to person for that very reason. Partners of N's do not always understand why this happens. They assume their N has the "traveling bug" or needs a change of scenery, so they continue to move around the globe with their N. If the N's partner is no longer providing NS for him, he will leave her, as well. Unconquered areas prove to be a valuable resource of NS for the N. That is why the Internet is so appealing to many N's.

The Internet provides anonymity and allows the N to reinvent himself as many times as necessary. The false self of an N can thrive on the Internet. It is no secret that Internet dating sites are crawling with personality-disordered people. Narcissists are no exception. An N's profile can read whatever he needs people to believe about him. On his quest to find the ideal mate, the N slowly sifts through all the possibilities. By chatting online with these individuals, the N gets to live out his false self and obtain the perfect relationship. When the "relationship" progresses beyond chatting, the N will sometimes ask for a phone number or suggest that he and his cyber pal meet in real life. N's will travel for miles, sometimes boarding planes or trains, to meet their new supply. The possibility of having found that *perfect mate* makes it easy to travel such distances. Besides, the rush the N gets from being able to live in his false self for an extended amount of time gives him the confidence he needs to take that next step. Such was the case of Barry, a divorced optician who was unofficially engaged to his partner of six months, Caitlin.

Caitlin and Barry

A mutual friend had introduced Caitlin and Barry just as Barry was recovering from his divorce. Barry was a handsome doctor who had the unfortunate habit of falling in love with the wrong type of woman. Barry was charming and became serious about Caitlin right away. Caitlin and Barry shared many common interests, and Barry exclaimed that he had finally found the woman of his dreams. Caitlin didn't feel exactly the same about Barry, but she felt that with time she could learn to care as much for Barry as he seemed to care for her. Besides, he lavished her with attention and was constantly complimenting her. Caitlin was attractive and was used to compliments, but Barry seemed to be more sincere with his compliments than had the men in her past. After six months of a relationship Barry moved in with Caitlin, promising to make their engagement official as soon as he found the perfect ring for his perfect woman.

Weeks after Barry moved in, Caitlin noticed he was spending more time on the computer and less time with her. When she questioned him about it, he became indignant and made her feel guilty for robbing him of his privacy. "If we are going to be married, you're going to have to back off and allow me my personal space," he would tell her. Eventually Barry no longer complimented Caitlin and he seemed to find fault with her at every turn. Caitlin became suspicious of all the time Barry spent online and had spyware installed on her computer so she could see what sites Barry was visiting. She was shocked to see that

Barry had been posting his profile on several dating sites. He had even used pictures of himself that Caitlin had taken on their vacation. He seemed reluctant to pose for her in his skimpy bathing suit, but said he could do it since they were "for her eyes only." Caitlin was also surprised to see that Barry had placed a picture of himself with full frontal nudity onto one of the sites that offered indiscrete profiles of its members. As she sat reading Barry's profiles, her eyes filled with tears. She couldn't believe what she was reading about the man she thought she knew. In one profile, Barry described himself as someone who knew very little about children and didn't want to date anyone who had kids. Barry had children from his first marriage and seemed to adore Caitlin's eight-year-old daughter. He was always telling her he wanted more children with her and that they would be so beautiful since both he and Caitlin had curly hair and dark skin.

Apparently, Barry had been visiting the dating sites long before he and Caitlin had decided to move in together. Many of the things Barry listed about himself were things he had never mentioned to Caitlin.

Barry had been sending emails to Gail, a woman whom he had met on one of the websites. Some of those emails were very intimate and graphic. He also mentioned Caitlin in a few of the emails, referring to her as a "friend." He hid the fact that he and Caitlin had been in an "exclusive relationship" for more than six months or that they were "unofficially engaged." Caitlin's daughter, whom Barry referred to as his own when talking with Caitlin, was not mentioned once. After reading those emails, Caitlin was horrified and wounded.

Caitlin confronted Barry when he returned home from work. She knew she had cornered him and felt she would finally hear the truth. However, her plan backfired as Barry began accusing her of invading his privacy and snooping around. He attacked her saying this was why he could never marry a woman like her. He said that she was too insecure to trust anyone and didn't have a life of her own so she had to become overly involved in his. She was no

better than his ex-wife. At least she had not been a snoop. Finally he yelled,
"Why is it that I'm always attracted to basket cases? Why am I being pun-
ished?"

He moved in with his friend Ted until he could get his own place, since
Barry had lost the lease on his old apartment and had nowhere to go. Of course,
Barry didn't mention his little incident to his new cyber pal Gail. He told her
that one of his friends had betrayed him and that he didn't feel like discussing
it. Once again, Barry proclaimed that at last his searching was over…no more
being caught up in relationships with evil women.

Because relocating to different areas eventually diminishes the playing
field of the N, the internet becomes desirable as an endless supply of territory.
When a "relationship" doesn't seem to be taking the turn the N expects, all he
has to do is click a button and the supply is forever blocked from him. And since
he doesn't always give truthful statistics on his profile, the N is virtually
untraceable. Cyber Narcissists are dangerous predators, but their endless source
of internet supply also makes it dangerous for the N. Without a decrease in sup-
ply, the N is less likely to get to a low enough point in his life to admit he has a
problem.

While N's are attracted to strength and confidence, they don't fool them-
selves into believing an almost perfect person would be attracted to them.
Therefore, they search for partners that have strength in certain areas, but who
may not be very attractive…or who may have insecurities about their careers or
amount of education. The N tries to convince his partner that he is looking past
what other men might notice and "loving them anyway." Sometimes an N will
say such things as, "I have treated you better than any other man has ever
treated you." The N assumes this to be true given the flaw in his partner that he
has so graciously "overlooked." In spite of her "flaw," the N's partner actually
possesses positive characteristics and is usually very confident at the onset of
their relationship. However, after being devalued by the N, the partner becomes

insecure about herself, feels self critical and lacks confidence. Confidence in a soon-to-be discarded partner is the usual attack strategy of an N when he or she is almost ready to move on. The impetus of the victim's horrified reaction to the attack gives the N the final energy he or she needs to make the break he or she was going to make anyway.

Chapter 18

Can N's Recover?

Whether you feel anger, disgust, pity or sorrow for your N, eventually you may wonder if there is hope for his or her recovery from NPD. Most experts in the field of psychology agree that there is no cure for NPD, only treatments for its symptoms. So it is understandable that the N sometimes realizes that something is not quite right with him or her, but the N never really accepts responsibility for any of it. Instead, the N rationalizes that the negatives in his or her personality are actually okay and that fate or his or her poor choices for partners are the problems.

Because the N chooses to believe in a "false" self, the Narcissist lacks the introspection necessary to become aware of any faults the person may possess. This makes it more difficult for the N to accept the possibility that he or she has a disorder.

Rather than seeing his faults as symptoms of a personality disorder, he interprets them "narcissistically." He views being rude or cruel to others as a strength that enables him to eliminate inefficiencies. His abusive actions are self-interpreted as ways to educate or enlighten. He considers his bouts of rage to be understandable acts of frustration brought on by the actions of less-evolved human beings.

These misinterpretations of his actions allow him to glorify his disorder and guard it as part of his self-esteem. An N must feel "special" and the "uniqueness" of his "false" self reinforces his belief in that. Therefore, if anyone tries to destroy his "false" self, they threaten to take away his source of power...his power to control those around him. He realizes that the destruction of his "false" self would reduce him to the lowly status of mediocrity, thus tossing him into an unknown world. The same fears that drive a co-dependent to stay in an abusive relationship (even though she is unhappy) drive the N to remain in the familiar world of his disorder, regardless of the pain he suffers. While the co-dependent is very emotionally attached to her N, the N is only emotionally attached to one thing, his disorder. This is why it so difficult for the N to work through many of the real problems of the disorder.

Of course, the first step toward healing NPD would be for the N to accept that she has the disorder. The second step would be for her to *want* to rid herself of the disorder even though that would mean giving up her familiar lifestyle and self-created universe.

If an N ever makes it to step two, he increases his chances of resolving his symptoms. Unfortunately, the very nature of an N prevents him from believing anything is wrong with him, even though he at times has feelings to the contrary. Therefore, it is almost impossible for an N to reach the second step toward overcoming his abominable behavior.

Sigmund Freud's theory of personality development explains that personality is comprised of three parts: the Id, the Ego, and the Super Ego. He described the Id as the foundation...our unconscious drives or instincts. The Ego is our conscious desires searching for ways to satisfy the wishes of the Id. And the Super Ego has two parts, the conscience, an internalization of punishments and warnings, and the ego ideal, which derives from rewards and positive models. The Super Ego represents society. Because an N views society (people from whom he extracts supply, while envying them and despising them for his dependence upon them) as "the enemy," he often appears as if he is without a Super Ego or that it is sadistic, malformed and immature due to the bad parenting he received. This is another reason a cure for NPD is viewed as so difficult.

But personality development does not have an expiration date. Although some parts of the personality are genetic, many parts are influenced by environment, society, and traumatic events. These are "life-changing" incidents. In the case of the N, what it should really be called is a "personality-changing" incident. Many things can lead to a person's resignation or desire to make changes in his/her personality. For an N, it is usually a huge task, because he is without supply and suffering extreme amounts of narcissistic injury when he feels desperate enough to admit he could possibly benefit from therapy.

Once in therapy, the N often reverts to his "charming self," and fishes for supply. If he can charm his therapist and gain supply, he will rebuild his unrealistic selfish self and justify his "misconstrued ideas" about needing therapy by believing they were based on his previous feelings of vulnerability. If his therapist *doesn't* offer him the type of supply he is seeking, he may become angry or irritated and devalue the therapist as someone who cannot benefit him, thus refusing help. There is a possibility, however, that after being refused narcissistic supply by his therapist, the N resigns himself to working through his problems in therapy, in desperate hope of being released from his disorder.

Freud said that the goal of therapy was to make the unconscious conscious. The N isn't aware of why he feels the way he does or why he reacts in particular ways. Through therapy, however, once he becomes aware of those unconscious motivations and reactions, he can learn to *modify* his behavior.

The types of therapy usually offered to an N often deal with "behavioral modifications." N's are taught to see the abuse they inflict upon others through the victim's eyes. An N has instincts that cause him to act insensitively or cruel, so he is taught in therapy not to act upon those first instincts. By learning to think and respond rather than react on impulse, the N can modify certain behaviors and avoid conflicts.

To believe that there is no cure for personality disorders discounts the possibility of continued personality change... and divine intervention. Believers in God feel he can snatch a dying, diseased person from the jowls of death; erasing all traces of his/her illness. If so, then N's can also be healed.

What some psychologists describe as behavioral patterns passed on by one's parents, the Bible refers to as "generational curses." Regardless of the terminology, the outcome is the same. One passage in the Bible asserts that the "sins of the father" are passed onto the sons. We see examples of this when we read about child molesters that claim to have been molested by their own parents...or generations of alcoholics, child abusers, etc. From a psychological viewpoint, some children repeat their parents' behaviors *subconsciously*. Sometimes the victims of abusers tell themselves they will be different than their abusers were and not succumb to the same addiction. Someone may refuse to drink alcohol if his parent was an alcoholic, yet may still possess some of the characteristics of an alcoholic becoming isolated, moody and depressed.

One method to cure a problem is to stop the pattern or break the curse. Nevertheless, many people live in denial, refusing to believe that they are continuing behaviors of their parents. While they refrain from actually hitting their children in order to be different from their physically abusive parents, some people may still evoke similar fears in their own children by verbally abusing their children, expressing intimidating attitudes toward them. Therefore, acceptance of the problem is important.

Next, an abused victim who does not want to perpetuate the behavior must refuse to continue living in such a way as to prevent the past from controlling the future. This problem can be avoided one step at a time. For example, if the victim's parents were the type to ignore him, never attending school functions or sporting activities, he can make a conscious effort to attend the activities of his own children. If her parents never helped with homework or spent time reviewing the child's day, she can make time even if exhausted from work to talk and be available. At first, these corrections will take effort and discipline on the N's part. But before long they will become more natural and he or she will begin to feel a sense of empowerment as the N takes control of changing the patterns.

Consciously changing behavior is only one part of the solution. When behavior modification is taught to people suffering from NPD, it is used as a way to *cope* with their disorder, not become cured of it. Therefore, behavior modification is important but not the cure. An N also needs to ask him or herself the question "why" concerning feelings, reactions and behaviors. The N should find out why he/she feels angry toward his/her child when the child reveals a family problem to a teacher. Why does an N find it necessary to convince others that *their* way is the right way? Many times we take our behavior for granted. When we express anger about something, we often feel justified in that expression. Obviously someone did something to provoke us. But when we ask ourselves why the situation provoked us to anger initially and try to grasp our own reasoning and motivation, we begin to understand ourselves.

By understanding ourselves we will be able to understand some of the negative behaviors passed on by parents or caregivers.

Perhaps the fears have been taught by our parents and we unknowingly received the "generational curse"; this may have caused us to lash out in anger at our child for "exposing our true selves"...for showing that we weren't the "good parent," the "great provider." Perhaps the image we wanted to project to the public was threatened by our child's retaliatory retorts. By asking "why," we are able to trace the origins of our behavior and consciously correct it. Making these corrections frees us from the destructive patterns of behavior or breaks the generational curse.

Whether you choose to interpret these actions as a "mindful" approach to self-healing or a conscious decision to break a generational curse, the important thing is that once the corrections are made, the effects of the disorder can be minimized. So, the good news is that it *is* possible for an N to improve!

We hope you have gained some insights that will allow you to resolve and/or improve your situation. Remember that all life-experiences can be used to help us become better, stronger people if used correctly. Learning why you are drawn to certain people and why you allow yourself to stay with them can help you avoid these situations in the future. Realizing that you may have been involved with someone who suffers from NPD can give you understanding that allows you to take his or her actions less personally, feel a certain amount of pity, or find ways to deal with the person, if you are going to stay.

Whether you decide to leave or stay on with your N, you may want to celebrate. You have learned the most important lessons of this book: to value yourself and to chart your own future course. You don't even have to invite anyone to join you in the celebration; you now know you are in very good company alone! And we wish you well on your continued journey of healing and discovery.

Bibliography

Beattie, Melodie. *Codependent No More: How to Stop Controlling Others and Start Caring for Yourself.* Hazledon Corporation, 1992.

Diagnostic and Statistical Manual of Mental Disorders, DSM-IV-TR Fourth Edition. American Psychiatric Association, 2000.

Miller, Alice. *The Drama of the Gifted Child.* Basic Books, Inc., 1981.

Pipher, Mary, Ph.D. *Reviving Ophelia: Saving the Selves of Adolescent Girls.* Penguin Group, 1992.

Vaknin, Sam, Ph.D. *Malignant Self Love: Narcissism Revisited.* Narcissus Publications, 1999-2006.